THE ULTIMATE MOVIE TRIVIA CHALLENGE

OVER 600 QUIZ QUESTIONS AND FUN
FACTS FOR MOVIE LOVERS ABOUT
FANTASTIC FILMS FROM THE 70S
TO THE PRESENT

BILL O'NEILL

CONTENTS

DON'T FORGET:
TWO FREE BOOKS

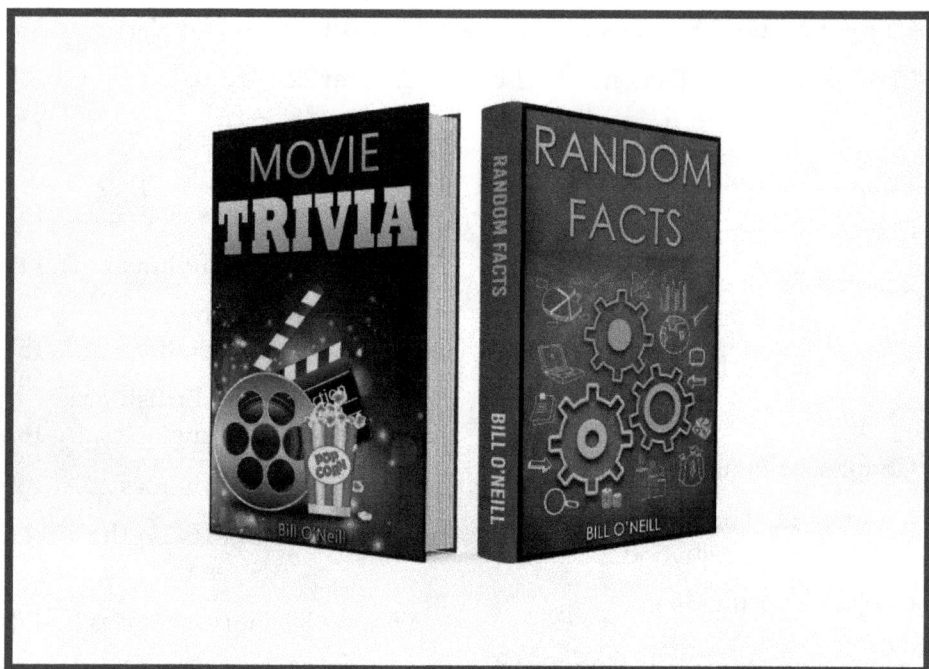

INTRODUCTION

So, you call yourself a movie buff. Let's put that to the test, shall we? Question one. In *The Lion King*, what was the name of Simba's uncle?

Okay, that's an easy one to start with. As any Disney fan knows, Simba's uncle was Scar. So, let's try something tougher.

Which British actor provided the voice for Simba's uncle Scar? Here's a hint — he had won the Best Actor Oscar three years earlier.

So…well done if you got that one right — it was Jeremy Irons! And finally, round three. Speaking of Jeremy Irons, what was the title of that 1990 movie for which he won the Oscar?

Phew! That's a tough one. It was *Reversal of Fortune*.

So, how did you fare? A positively stellar three out of three? More importantly, though, have these few warm-up questions inspired you to test your movie trivia knowledge even further? If so, you're in the right place.

This is *The Ultimate Movie Trivia Challenge* — a compendium of more than 600 movie questions, all specially put together to test your cinema knowledge to its limit. The questions here cover more than a century of moviemaking, and they take in all the major movie genres. Each topic has its own chapter, so feel free to jump right into whatever genre or movie style you like the most. Alternatively, of course, just work your way through the book, one 18-question quiz at a time.

Be sure to keep track of your total scores as you go, of course, so you can find out if you truly are a movie buff!

CHAPTER 1
PREQUELS & SEQUELS

We're getting things started here with a chapter all about opening stories, follow-ups, and franchises — prequels and sequels!

1. What was the subtitle of *Episode I*, the first of the *Star Wars* prequels, released in 1999?

    a. Revenge of the Sith
    b. A New Hope
    c. The Phantom Menace
    d. Attack of the Clones

2. *Here We Go Again* was the 2018 sequel to what 2008 blockbuster?

    a. *Mamma Mia!*
    b. *Madagascar*
    c. *Sex and the City*
    d. *Kung Fu Panda*

3. 2012's *Prometheus* was part of what long-running sci-fi franchise?

    a. *Predator*
    b. *X-Men*
    c. *The Planet of the Apes*
    d. *Alien*

4. What was the only movie in the *Harry Potter* franchise split into two parts?

    a. *The Deathly Hallows*
    b. *The Half-Blood Prince*
    c. *The Goblet of Fire*
    d. *The Order of the Phoenix*

5. In the 1935 sequel to Boris Karloff's *Frankenstein*, who played the bride in *Bride of Frankenstein*?

    a. Angela Lansbury
    b. Elsa Lanchester
    c. Margaret Rutherford
    d. Hermione Gingold

6. Who returned to the *Nightmare on Elm Street* franchise in 1993 to direct *New Nightmare*?

    a. Sam Raimi
    b. John Carpenter
    c. George A. Romero
    d. Wes Craven

7. What was the 1997 sequel to *Jurassic Park*?

    a. *The Lost World*
    b. *The Lost Kingdom*
    c. *The Lost Island*
    d. *The Lost Mountain*

8. Put these George A. Romero zombie movies in order, starting with the oldest:

    a. *Land of the Dead*
    b. *Day of the Dead*
    c. *Dawn of the Dead*
    d. *Night of the Living Dead*

9. The first sequel ever to win the Academy Award for Best Picture was the second film in what series?

    a. *Lord of the Rings*
    b. *The Godfather*
    c. *Rocky*
    d. *Toy Story*

10. Which comic actor voiced the character Stinky Pete in *Toy Story 2*?

    a. Ted Danson
    b. Mike Myers
    c. Kelsey Grammer
    d. Jim Carrey

11. What was the title of the fourth *Mission: Impossible* movie?

    a. *Fallout*
    b. *Dead Reckoning*
    c. *Final Reckoning*
    d. *Ghost Protocol*

12. 1997's sci-fi blockbuster *Alien Resurrection* was the … ?

    a. … second film in the series
    b. … third film in the series
    c. … fourth film in the series
    d. … fifth film in the series

13. Who played Clubber Lang in *Rocky III*?

    a. Carl Weathers
    b. Dolph Lundgren

c. Tommy Morrison

d. Mr. T

14. In what year was *Avengers: Endgame* released?

    a. 2015

    b. 2017

    c. 2019

    d. 2021

15. Who was the main villain in 2004's *Spider-Man 2*?

    a. The Green Goblin

    b. Doctor Octopus

    c. Sandman

    d. Venom

16. Which of these blockbuster sequels of the 1990s was released first?

    a. *Terminator 2: Judgment Day*

    b. *Die Hard with a Vengeance*

    c. *Scream 2*

    d. *Ace Ventura: When Nature Calls*

17. In what city is *Home Alone 2* set?

    a. Paris

    b. London

    c. New York

    d. Chicago

18. *The New Batch* was the 1990 sequel to what 1980s creature feature?

    a. *Tremors*

    b. *Gremlins*

    c. *Piranha*

    d. *The Fly*

ANSWERS

1. C. *The Phantom Menace. Episode I* grossed almost $1 billion upon its release in the spring of 1999.
2. A. *Mamma Mia!* The 2018 sequel *Here We Go Again* took the *Mamma Mia!* franchise's total gross past $1 billion.
3. D. *Alien.* Partly telling the origin story of the *Alien* xenomorphs, *Prometheus* marked the return of the franchise's creator and first director, Ridley Scott.
4. A. *The Deathly Hallows.* The final book in JK Rowling's *Harry Potter* series was so long that the movie adaptation was split into two installments in 2010 and 2011.
5. B. Elsa Lanchester. Besides her iconic role in *The Bride of Frankenstein,* Lanchester is perhaps best known for her role as Katie Nanny in 1964's *Mary Poppins.*
6. D. Wes Craven. Having first created the character of Freddy Krueger way back in 1984, Craven returned to the franchise in 1994.
7. A. *The Lost World.* If you said *Lost Kingdom,* you might be getting it confused with 2018's *Jurassic World: Fallen Kingdom!*
8. D. *Night of the Living Dead* (1968), C. *Dawn of the Dead* (1978), B. *Day of the Dead* (1985), and A. *Land of the Dead* (2005). *Night of the Living Dead* was remade in 1990, but not by Romero.
9. B. *The Godfather.* Francis Ford Coppola initially wasn't interested in writing a sequel to 1972's Best Picture winner *The Godfather,* but *The Godfather: Part II* went on to win the same award as its predecessor in 1974.
10. C. Kelsey Grammer. Best known for playing the title character on TV's *Frasier,* Kelsey Grammer played the part of a duplicitous elderly prospector toy in the 1999 sequel to *Toy Story.*
11. D. *Ghost Protocol. Mission: Impossible IV* was the first film in the series to get a subtitle, following *Mission: Impossible* (1996), *Mission Impossible 2* (2000), and *Mission: Impossible III* (2006).
12. C. ... fourth film in the series. The film was directed by Jean-Pierre Jeunet.
13. D. Mr. T. Carl Weathers played Rocky's opponent Apollo Creed in the first two *Rocky* movies, with Mr. T taking over as the main adversary for the third in 1982.
14. C. 2019. *Endgame* followed 2018's *Infinity War,* 2015's *Age of Ultron,* and 2012's *The Avengers.*

15. B. Doctor Octopus. All four of the villains here appeared in Sam Raimi's *Spider-Man* series.
16. A. *Terminator 2: Judgment Day.* James Cameron's follow-up to *The Terminator* was released in 1991; *Die Hard with a Vengeance* and *Ace Ventura: When Nature Calls* in 1995; and *Scream 2* in 1997.
17. C. New York. The film's full title was *Home Alone: Lost in New York.*
18. B. *Gremlins.* Both movies in the horror-comedy *Gremlins* series were directed by Joe Dante.

DID YOU KNOW?

The very first movie sequel in history is said to be *The Fall of a Nation* — the 1916 follow-up to the silent epic *The Birth of a Nation.*

CHAPTER 2
THE '20S & '30S

We're taking things right back to the beginning in this chapter, with a set of questions dedicated to the movies and movie stars of the 1920s and '30s.

1. Which Hollywood studio produced a series of monster movies in the 1930s, including *Frankenstein*, *The Mummy*, and *The Invisible Man*?

    a. Warner Bros.
    b. MGM
    c. Universal
    d. United Artists

2. Which silent era entertainer starred in the movies *The Gold Rush* and *Modern Times*?

    a. Harold Lloyd
    b. Charlie Chaplin
    c. Buster Keaton
    d. Douglas Fairbanks

3. What kind of monster is the subject of the classic 1922 silent movie *Nosferatu*?

    a. Werewolf
    b. Giant
    c. Sea monster
    d. Vampire

4. For which 1930s movie did Hattie McDaniel become the first African-American Oscar-winner?

    a. *Chicago*
    b. *Jezebel*
    c. *Gone with the Wind*
    d. *You Can't Take It with You*

5. Who directed the 1927 silent epic *Metropolis*?

    a. F.W. Murnau
    b. Erich von Stroheim
    c. King Vidor
    d. Fritz Lang

6. What was the very first movie to win the Academy Award for Best Picture back in 1929?

    a. *The Jazz Singer*
    b. *The Great Dictator*

c. *Wings*

d. *The Way of All Flesh*

7. Which of these early classics was released first?

a. *Battleship Potemkin*

b. *King Kong*

c. *Dracula*

d. *Duck Soup*

8. Who made his Hollywood debut in a 1939 adaptation of *Wuthering Heights*?

a. Charles Laughton

b. Laurence Olivier

c. John Mills

d. Ralph Richardson

9. What is the name of the island on which King Kong lives?

a. Bone Island

b. Heart Island

c. Eye Island

d. Skull Island

10. Who took on the role later played by Judy Garland, Barbra Streisand, and Lady Gaga in the original *A Star is Born* in 1937?

a. Janet Gaynor

b. Bette Davis

c. Vivien Leigh

d. Joan Crawford

11. What nationality was Bela Lugosi, the star of the 1931 horror classic *Dracula*?

a. Romanian

b. Hungarian

c. Danish

d. German

12. In *The Wizard of Oz*, what state does Dorothy Gale live in before traveling to Oz?

a. Missouri

b. Oklahoma

c. Georgia

d. Kansas

13. Which of these is the title of a classic 1931 mystery thriller?

    a. *K*
    b. *L*
    c. *M*
    d. *N*

14. Who made his feature film directorial debut with the 1925 silent movie, *The Pleasure Garden*?

    a. John Ford
    b. Alfred Hitchcock
    c. Frank Capra
    d. Orson Welles

15. Which George Bernard Shaw play was adapted for film in 1938, starring Leslie Howard?

    a. *Pygmalion*
    b. *Man and Superman*
    c. *Caesar and Cleopatra*
    d. *Arms and the Man*

16. After winning the Best Actress Academy Award in 1939, who went on to be nominated for the same award every year until 1943, becoming the first person nominated for an acting Oscar in five consecutive years?

    a. Vivien Leigh
    b. Katharine Hepburn
    c. Greta Garbo
    d. Bette Davis

17. As whom did Adriana Caselotti become famous in 1930s Hollywood?

    a. The Wicked Witch of the West in *The Wizard of Oz*
    b. Snow White in *Snow White and the Seven Dwarfs*
    c. Scarlett O'Hara in *Gone with the Wind*
    d. Ann Darrow in *King Kong*

18. True or False? When he starred in *The Adventures of Robin Hood* in 1938, Errol Flynn became the first person in movie history to play Robin on film.

ANSWERS

1. C. Universal. The so-called Universal Monsters franchise began way back in 1913, with a silent adaptation of Robert Louis Stevenson's classic horror novel, *Dr. Jekyll and Mr. Hyde*.
2. B. Charlie Chaplin. Chaplin reportedly thought 1925's *The Gold Rush* to be his greatest film, and it remains the most successful comedy movie of the silent era.
3. D. Vampire. Subtitled *A Symphony of Horror*, F.W. Murnau's *Nosferatu* was released in 1922. Although the vampire in question is named Count Orlock in Murnau's film, the movie was an entirely unauthorized adaptation of Bram Stoker's *Dracula*, which had been published just 25 years earlier.
4. C. *Gone with the Wind*. McDaniel's victory was even more extraordinary given that segregation was still in place in the United States at the time. She had even been prohibited from attending the premiere of *Gone with the Wind* in Atlanta.
5. D. Fritz Lang. *Metropolis* took almost a year and a half to film, and it runs more than two and a half hours in length.
6. C. *Wings*. World War I epic *Wings* took home the inaugural Best Picture Oscar (then known as the award for Outstanding Picture) at the first Academy Awards in February 1929.
7. A. *Battleship Potemkin*. While the other three movies are from the 1930s, *Battleship Potemkin* was released in 1925.
8. B. Laurence Olivier. Having appeared in British movies for almost a decade, *Wuthering Heights* was Olivier's Hollywood debut.
9. D. Skull Island. The inhabitants of Skull Island were made using stop-motion animation in the original 1933 movie.
10. A. Janet Gaynor. Gaynor starred opposite acclaimed actor Fredric March in the original *A Star is Born*, for which they both received Oscar nominations.
11. B. Hungarian. Lugosi was an acclaimed stage actor in his native Hungary before emigrating to America in the 1920s.
12. D. Kansas. Although *The Wizard of Oz* is credited to director Victor Fleming, most of the Kansas scenes were filmed by King Vidor, as Fleming was called away mid-filming to assist on *Gone with the Wind*.
13. C. *M*. Directed by Fritz Lang, *M* starred Peter Lorre as serial killer Hans Beckert.

14. B. Alfred Hitchcock. Hitchcock began his pre-Hollywood career with a string of silent movies in Europe, including his first thriller, *The Lodger*, in 1927.
15. A. *Pygmalion*. George Bernard Shaw adapted his own play for the big screen, winning the Academy Award for Adapted Screenplay in the process.
16. D. Bette Davis. Davis won both her Best Actress Oscars in the 1930s, in 1936 and 1939. Besides her five consecutive nominations from 1939 to 1943, she also received nominations in 1945, 1951, 1953, and 1963, becoming the first person to attain ten acting Oscar nods.
17. B. Snow White in *Snow White and the Seven Dwarfs*. Hollywood actress and singer Adriana Caselotti provided the voice for Snow White in Walt Disney's first feature-length animated movie in 1937. Margaret Hamilton played the Wicked Witch, Vivien Leigh starred as Scarlett O'Hara, and the first Ann Darrow in *King Kong* was Fay Wray.
18. False. The first known movie adaptation of the *Robin Hood* story was a silent short in 1908; Flynn wasn't even the first feature-length Robin Hood, as Douglas Fairbanks had played the character more than a decade earlier, in 1922.

DID YOU KNOW?

Douglas Fairbanks' *Robin Hood* was the first film in history to receive a gala Hollywood premiere, held at Grauman's Egyptian Theatre on October 18, 1922.

CHAPTER 3
SCIENCE FICTION

As modern as it might seem, science fiction has been part of the movie world since the very earliest days of cinema — and the questions in this round cover almost that entire history of the genre!

1. Who starred in Steven Spielberg's 2005 adaptation of *The War of the Worlds*?

   a. Tom Hanks
   b. Tom Cruise
   c. Will Smith
   d. Brad Pitt

2. What science fiction movie series is based on a 1963 novel by the French author Pierre Boulle?

   a. *Alien*
   b. *Planet of the Apes*
   c. *Blade Runner*
   d. *The Terminator*

3. Put these four science fiction classics in order, earliest to latest:

   a. *2001: A Space Odyssey*
   b. *Alien*
   c. *The Thing*
   d. *Forbidden Planet*

4. How old was Drew Barrymore when she starred in Steven Spielberg's *E.T. the Extra Terrestrial*?

   a. Three
   b. Six
   c. Nine
   d. 12

5. Which Star Trek cast member directed Star Trek III: The Search for Spock in 1984?

   a. William Shatner
   b. DeForest Kelley
   c. Leonard Nimoy
   d. George Takei

6. Which of these Oscar-winners does not appear in 2010's sci-fi epic *Inception*?

   a. Leonardo DiCaprio
   b. Michael Caine

c.   Marion Cotillard

d.   Will Smith

7.   Sci-fi classic *Forbidden Planet* was based on which Shakespeare play?

   a.   *The Taming of the Shrew*
   b.   *The Tempest*
   c.   *A Midsummer Night's Dream*
   d.   *A Comedy of Errors*

8.   Which of these 1970s sci-fi classics was a remake of an earlier 1950s movie?

   a.   *Invasion of the Body Snatchers*
   b.   *Close Encounters of the Third Kind*
   c.   *Logan's Run*
   d.   *Rollerball*

9.   *The Andromeda Strain*, a sci-fi thriller about a deadly pathogen from outer space, was based on a novel by which author?

   a.   Isaac Asimov
   b.   Steven Spielberg
   c.   Philip K. Dick
   d.   Michael Crichton

10.   Which singer starred in *Mad Max Beyond Thunderdome* in 1985?

   a.   Whitney Houston
   b.   Diana Ross
   c.   Tina Turner
   d.   Madonna

11.   Which actress appeared as Dr. Alice Krippin, the creator of a cure for cancer that turns into a mutational virus, in the 2007 sci-fi horror *I Am Legend*?

   a.   Emma Thompson
   b.   Judi Dench
   c.   Maggie Smith
   d.   Helena Bonham Carter

12.   What sci-fi classic features an alien named Klaatu?

   a.   *The War of the Worlds*
   b.   *The Day the Earth Stood Still*
   c.   *2001: A Space Odyssey*
   d.   *Blade Runner*

13. Which of these A-listers starred in *Parasite* director Bong Joon Ho's 2025 sci-fi comedy *Mickey 17*?

    a. Robert Pattinson
    b. Daniel Radcliffe
    c. Jacob Elordi
    d. Kieran Culkin

14. Steve McQueen, Jack Nicholson, Dustin Hoffman, and James Caan all reportedly turned down the lead role in what 1977 sci-fi hit — with Richard Dreyfuss going on to be cast instead?

    a. *Star Wars*
    b. *Rollerball*
    c. *Close Encounters of the Third Kind*
    d. *The Man Who Fell to Earth*

15. In the 1985 movie, how fast does the DeLorean have to go in order to travel *Back to the Future*?

    a. 55 miles per hour
    b. 66 miles per hour
    c. 77 miles per hour
    d. 88 miles per hour

16. Who directed the sci-fi classics *RoboCop* and *Total Recall*?

    a. John Hughes
    b. Robert Zemeckis
    c. Paul Verhoeven
    d. Wolfgang Petersen

17. Who was nominated for an Oscar for her lead role in the space thriller *Gravity* in 2013?

    a. Sandra Bullock
    b. Angelina Jolie
    c. Scarlett Johannson
    d. Natalie Portman

18. What was the name of the character played by Vin Diesel in the *Pitch Black* movies?

    a. Roddick
    b. Riddick
    c. Benedick
    d. Medick

ANSWERS

1. B. Tom Cruise. Spielberg and Cruise reportedly so enjoyed working together on 2002's sci-fi caper *Minority Report* that they immediately began looking for another science fiction thriller and chose *The War of the Worlds* as their next project.
2. B. *Planet of the Apes*. The series began with the 1968 adaptation of Boulle's novel *La Planète des singes*.
3. D. *Forbidden Planet* (1956), A. *2001: A Space Odyssey* (1968), B. *Alien* (1979), C. *The Thing* (1982).
4. B. Six. Barrymore's role as Gertie in 1982'S *E.T.* was only her second acting role.
5. C. Leonard Nimoy. Spock actor Leonard Nimoy also directed *Star Trek IV: The Voyage Home* in 1986, while William Shatner directed *Star Trek V: The Final Frontier* in 1989.
6. D. Will Smith. Both Will Smith and fellow Oscar-winner Brad Pitt were offered the lead role in Christopher Nolan's *Inception,* which eventually went to Leonardo DiCaprio.
7. B. *The Tempest*. The 1956 classic relocated Shakespeare's tale of a shipwrecked crew washed up on a magical island to outer space.
8. A. *Invasion of the Body Snatchers*. Based on a novel by the American author Jack Finney, *Invasion of the Body Snatchers* had already been made in 1956 before the 1978 remake starring Donald Sutherland.
9. D. Michael Crichton. Best known for writing *Jurassic Park*, Crichton's novel *The Andromeda Strain* was adapted for the screen by Robert Wise in 1971.
10. C. Tina Turner. Turner, who played Aunty Entity in the third *Mad Max* movie, also recorded two songs for the movie, "One of the Living" and "We Don't Need Another Hero."
11. A. Emma Thompson. Thompson appears on screen only briefly in the movie, in an on-screen television interview, and goes uncredited for her performance.
12. B. *The Day the Earth Stood Still*. Klaatu is the name of the extraterrestrial who arrives on Earth in an attempt to convince humanity to change its ways.
13. A. Robert Pattinson. He plays the title role in *Mickey 17*, a menial worker who is cloned every time he dies.

14. C. *Close Encounters of the Third Kind*. Steve McQueen was reportedly director Steven Spielberg's first choice, but *Jaws* star Richard Dreyfuss eventually won the part.
15. D. 88 miles per hour. Ironically, the original DeLorean car could in reality only go at 85.
16. C. Paul Verhoeven. As well as *RoboCop* and *Total Recall*, Verhoeven also directed sci-fi classic *Starship Troopers*.
17. A. Sandra Bullock. All the other answers here were either considered for or offered the role.
18. B. Riddick. Vin Diesel has played Riddick in all four *Pitch Black* movies, including the original movie's 2004 sequel, *The Chronicles of Riddick*.

DID YOU KNOW?

The very first sci-fi movie was 1902's *A Trip to the Moon*.

CHAPTER 4
HISTORICAL EPICS

The century-long history of Hollywood has produced movies covering millennia of history—all of which is the subject of this next set of questions.

1. Before he was famous, which future Hollywood director served as secondary assistant director during the famous chariot race in 1959's *Ben-Hur*?

   a. Henry Ford
   b. Sergio Leone
   c. Alfred Hitchcock
   d. Stanley Kubrick

2. Who directed *Gladiator*?

   a. David Fincher
   b. Ridley Scott
   c. Paul Thomas Anderson
   d. James Cameron

3. Who received a record $1 million fee to play the title role in the notorious 1963 epic *Cleopatra*?

   a. Joan Crawford
   b. Elizabeth Taylor
   c. Katharine Hepburn
   d. Audrey Hepburn

4. Which of these 2000s historical epics had the subtitle *The Far Side of the World*?

   a. *In the Heart of the Sea*
   b. *Master and Commander*
   c. *Dunkirk*
   d. *Troy*

5. Who was the only member of the cast of *The Deer Hunter* to win an Academy Award for their performance?

   a. Robert De Niro
   b. Christopher Walken
   c. John Cazale
   d. Meryl Streep

6. Who played Moses in 1956's epic retelling of the story of Exodus, *The Ten Commandments*?

a. Charlton Heston
b. Burt Lancaster
c. Peter Ustinov
d. Yul Brenner

7. Who played *Napoleon* in Ridley Scott's 2023 epic?

a. Cillian Murphy
b. Joaquin Phoenix
c. Rupert Everett
d. Russell Crowe

8. Which legendary actor starred opposite Brad Pitt and Orlando Bloom in Wolfgang Petersen's *Troy* in 2004?

a. Peter O'Toole
b. Ian McKellen
c. Derek Jacobi
d. Anthony Hopkins

9. Which actor underwent weeks of wilderness training in rural Alabama in preparation for his role in 1992's *The Last of the Mohicans*?

a. Tom Hanks
b. Daniel Day-Lewis
c. Jack Nicholson
d. Sean Penn

10. Who directed 1965's three-hour Russian war epic *Doctor Zhivago*?

a. Robert Wise
b. John Ford
c. David Lean
d. Ingmar Bergman

11. Winner of seven Academy Awards, where and when is the 1957 epic *The Bridge on the River Kwai* set?

a. Medieval Japan
b. 1920s China
c. 19th century Thailand
d. World War II Burma

12. Which actor starred opposite Liam Neeson as concentration camp commandant Amon Göth in the Oscar-winning epic *Schindler's List*?

a. Kenneth Branagh
b. Tom Courtenay

c. Pete Postlethwaite

d. Ralph Fiennes

13. To what war-torn European nation are the German soldiers in World War I epic *All Quiet on the Western Front* sent?

a. France

b. Russia

c. Austria

d. Italy

14. How many Oscars did *Titanic* win from a record 14 nominations?

a. Eight

b. Ning

c. Ten

d. 11

15. Which of these Hollywood legends did not appear in Stanley Kubrick's 1960 epic *Spartacus*?

a. Kirk Douglas

b. Laurence Olivier

c. Tony Curtis

d. Charlton Heston

16. What Vietnam war epic is based on a novel by Joseph Conrad?

a. *Born on the Fourth of July*

b. *The Deer Hunter*

c. *Apocalypse Now*

d. *We Were Soldiers*

17. Whom did future *Man from U.N.C.L.E.* star David McCallum play in the 1965 Biblical epic *The Greatest Story Ever Told*?

a. Jesus

b. Judas

c. Herod

d. John the Baptist

18. Which of these Hollywood legends starred alongside the likes of John Wayne, Henry Fonda, and Gregory Peck in John Ford's 1962 all-star epic *How the West Was Won*?

a. James Stewart

b. Anthony Perkins

c. David Niven

d. Robert Mitchum

ANSWERS

1. B. Sergio Leone. Five years before the release of *A Fistful of Dollars*, Sergio Leone worked as an assistant to the second-unit directors on *Ben-Hur*.
2. B. Ridley Scott. Scott also directed 2024's follow-up, *Gladiator II*.
3. B. Elizabeth Taylor. Taylor's record salary was just one of a number of reasons why the movie's production eventually spiraled to more than $44 million (equivalent to around $430 million today!).
4. B. *Master and Commander*. Directed by Peter Weir, the movie starred Russell Crowe and Paul Bettany.
5. B. Christopher Walken. De Niro and Streep were both nominated for their performances, but Walken was the only winner that night, taking home the 1979 Oscar for Best Supporting Actor.
6. A. Charlton Heston. Directed and narrated by Cecil B. DeMille, *The Ten Commandments* was one of Hollywood's most ambitious movies, with a runtime of 220 minutes.
7. B. Joaquin Phoenix. Russell Crowe played the lead role in Ridley Scott's *Gladiator*, while Rupert Everett appeared as the Duke of Wellington in *Napoleon*.
8. A. Peter O'Toole. O'Toole played Priam, the King of Troy, in the film, alongside Brian Cox as Agamemnon.
9. B. Daniel Day-Lewis. He studied alongside US Army Special Forces personnel, learning how to use period weaponry, hunt game, and start fires.
10. C. David Lean. Lean went on to be nominated for an Oscar for the movie.
11. D. World War II Burma. *The Bridge on the River Kwai* won seven Oscars from eight nominations, including Best Picture, Director (David Lean), and Actor (Alec Guinness).
12. D. Ralph Fiennes. The movie also starred Ben Kingsley as Schindler's accountant, Itzhak Stern.
13. A. France. *All Quiet on the Western Front* is an adaptation of a semi-autobiographical novel by the German writer Erich Maria Remarque.
14. D. 11. The 14 Oscar nominations for *Titanic* tied the record set by *All About Eve* back in 1950; in winning 11, it equaled the same total won by *Ben-Hur* in 1959.

15. D. Charlton Heston. Kirk Douglas, who took the title role in *Spartacus*, reportedly began developing the movie when he lost out on the role of Ben Hur to Heston.
16. C. *Apocalypse Now*. Francis Ford Coppola's infamous Vietnam War drama was based on Conrad's 1899 novella, *Heart of Darkness*.
17. B. Judas. While McCallum took on the role of Judas Iscariot, Jesus was played by Max von Sydow, Herod by José Ferrer, and John the Baptist by Charlton Heston.
18. A. James Stewart. Running to almost three hours, *How the West Was Won* was a sprawling western saga covering the Gold Rush, the expansion of the railroads, and the American Civil War.

DID YOU KNOW?

Despite being the most successful movie of 1963, the production and promotion of *Cleopatra* was so expensive that the film barely made a profit.

CHAPTER 5
LEADING MEN

From Charlie Chaplin and the stars of the silent era to superheroes and dramatic heavyweights, the past century has seen some remarkable leading men grace the silver screen.

1. Which legendary actor's filmography includes *A Streetcar Named Desire, On the Waterfront,* and *Apocalypse Now*?
   a. Robert Duvall
   b. Al Pacino
   c. Marlon Brando
   d. Harrison Ford

2. Which of these Golden Age movie stars famously played the character Rick Blaine in a 1942 classic?
   a. Humphrey Bogart
   b. Frank Sinatra
   c. Gary Cooper
   d. James Stewart

3. Which leading man was nicknamed "The Duke"?
   a. Paul Newman
   b. Clint Eastwood
   c. Robert Redford
   d. John Wayne

4. Who took home his second Best Actor Academy Award in 2021, in a shock win that saw him become the oldest winner of an Oscar in any acting category, at the age of 83?
   a. Ian McKellen
   b. Christopher Plummer
   c. Anthony Hopkins
   d. Clint Eastwood

5. Who has played characters called Jack Torrance, Randle McMurphy, Frank Costello, and Jack Napier on the big screen?
   a. Jack Nicholson
   b. Sean Penn
   c. Christopher Walken
   d. Dennis Hopper

6. In which of his movies does James Stewart say the line, "You want the moon? Just say the word and I'll throw a lasso around it and pull it down"?

a. *Mr. Smith Goes to Washington*
b. *Vertigo*
c. *It's A Wonderful Life*
d. *Harvey*

7. True or False? Steve McQueen performed the famous motorcycle chase in *The Great Escape* himself.

   e. Who famously won back-to-back Best Actor Oscars in the 1990s?
   f. Nicholas Cage
   g. Tom Hanks
   h. Jack Nicholson
   i. Geoffrey Rush

8. Put these Hollywood Roberts in order from oldest to youngest:
   a. Robert De Niro
   b. Robert Pattinson
   c. Robert Redford
   d. Robert Downey, Jr.

9. Out of nine nominations, Al Pacino has only won one Oscar — for his role in which of his films?
   a. *The Godfather*
   b. *Serpico*
   c. *Dog Day Afternoon*
   d. *Scent of a Woman*

10. Which of these legendary leading men has not played Count Dracula on the big screen?
    a. Christopher Lee
    b. Anthony Hopkins
    c. Gary Oldman
    d. Frank Langella

11. Which Hollywood legend made his final on-screen appearance as a mob boss in 2002's *Road to Perdition*?
    a. Laurence Olivier
    b. Walter Matthau
    c. Alec Guinness
    d. Paul Newman

12. Which Oscar-nominated actor played a troubled teenager in the 2001 supernatural drama *Donnie Darko*?

a. James Franco
b. Jake Gyllenhaal
c. Chris Pine
d. Channing Tatum

13. Which leading man of Hollywood's Golden Age was born in Tasmania, Australia, in 1909?

a. Clark Gable
b. Rudolph Valentino
c. Charlie Chaplin
d. Errol Flynn

14. Who was the first person in the 21st century to be nominated for an Oscar for a performance in a big-screen adaptation of a Shakespeare play?

a. Denzel Washington
b. Ian McKellen
c. Kenneth Branagh
d. Leonardo DiCaprio

15. Which actor's roles have included twice playing the US president, once playing the US vice president, and twice playing God?

a. Michael Caine
b. Willem Defoe
c. Morgan Freeman
d. Alan Alda

16. Which legendary actor's co-stars include Audrey Hepburn in *Roman Holiday*, Ava Gardner in *The Snows of Kilimanjaro*, and Jean Simmons in *The Big Country*?

a. John Wayne
b. Steve McQueen
c. Elvis Presley
d. Gregory Peck

17. Whose film career includes roles in *The Fugitive, No Country for Old Men, and Men In Black*?

a. Will Smith
b. Harrison Ford
c. Rip Torn
d. Tommy Lee Jones

ANSWERS

1. C. Marlon Brando. Robert Duvall and Harrison Ford both starred alongside Brando in *Apocalypse Now*, while Al Pacino was Brando's co-star in *The Godfather* movies.
2. A. Humphrey Bogart. Rick Blaine was the character Bogart played in *Casablanca*.
3. D. John Wayne. According to legend, Wayne's nickname had nothing to do with his movie career: the Wayne family had a pet Airedale terrier named Duke when John was young, which soon became attached to him too.
4. C. Anthony Hopkins. Hopkins' second Best Actor win for 2020's *The Father* came as something of a surprise, as it had been widely presumed Chadwick Boseman would win posthumously for *Ma Rainey's Black Bottom*.
5. A. Jack Nicholson. Those are his roles in *The Shining*, *One Flew Over the Cuckoo's Nest*, *The Departed*, and *Batman* (Jack Napier is the real name of Jack Nicholson's Joker).
6. C. *It's A Wonderful Life*. Stewart's character, George, promises the moon to his girlfriend Mary in a memorable scene in this 1946 Christmas classic.
7. True. McQueen was an avid and skilled motorcyclist. The stunt drivers were only brought in to replace him for insurance purposes.
8. B. Tom Hanks. All four of these leading men were '90s Oscar winners, but only Tom Hanks won his two awards consecutively, for *Philadelphia* and *Forrest Gump* in 1993 and 1994.
9. C. Robert Redford (1936), A. Robert De Niro (1943), Robert Downey, Jr. (1965), Robert Pattinson (1986).
10. D. *Scent of a Woman*. Incredibly, Al Pacino's nominated roles span six decades, from *The Godfather* in 1973 to *The Irishman* in 2020.
11. B. Anthony Hopkins. Hopkins played Van Helsing opposite Gary Oldman's count in director Francis Ford Coppola's adaptation of Bram Stoker's *Dracula* in 1992.
12. D. Paul Newman. His performance also earned him his final Oscar nomination, for Best Supporting Actor. Newman's last major role was off-screen, voicing Doc Hudson in 2006's *Cars*.
13. B. Jake Gyllenhaal. Incredibly, Gyllenhaal had already been acting for ten years before his breakout role in *Donnie Darko* at the age of 21.

14. D. Errol Flynn. Having landed the role in an early dramatization of the *Mutiny on the Bounty*, Flynn first relocated from Australia to England, and then from England to Hollywood in the mid-1930s.
15. A. Denzel Washington. He took the 2000s' first Shakespearean Oscar nomination for his role in Joel Coen's adaptation of *The Tragedy of Macbeth* in 2021.
16. C. Morgan Freeman. Freeman played the president in both *Deep Impact* and *Angel Has Fallen*, played the vice president in *London Has Fallen*, and played God in both *Bruce Almighty* and *Evan Almighty*.
17. D. Gregory Peck. In a stellar career spanning seven decades, Gregory Peck worked in television, radio, and film, earning six Oscar nominations — and winning one — in the process.
18. D. Tommy Lee Jones. Tommy Lee Jones' role as Agent K in the *Men in Black* movies nearly went to Clint Eastwood (who was the studio's preferred choice), while Jones himself almost turned the part down because the original script — in his words! — "stank."

DID YOU KNOW?

It wasn't just the viewers who were shocked when Anthony Hopkins scooped his second Best Actor Oscar in 2021. The legendary actor himself was so certain that Chadwick Boseman was going to win that he did not travel to Los Angeles and instead stayed at home in Wales — and went to bed!

CHAPTER 6
ACTION & ADVENTURE

Action movies covering almost a century of Hollywood history are the topic of this next set of questions.

1. Which future Oscar-winner starred opposite Errol Flynn as Maid Marion in 1938's *The Adventures of Robin Hood*?

   a. Bette Davis
   b. Olivia de Havilland
   c. Joan Crawford
   d. Sofia Loren

2. What classic 1980s action movie is set almost entirely inside the fictional Nakatomi Plaza skyscraper?

   a. *Terminator*
   b. *Die Hard*
   c. *Mad Max*
   d. *Judge Dredd*

3. In what decade is the first *Indiana Jones* film, *Raiders of the Lost Ark*, set?

   a. 1910s
   b. 1920s
   c. 1930s
   d. 1940s

4. The notion of taking a red pill or a blue pill to either accept reality or live obliviously is based on a scene from what action movie?

   a. *Aliens*
   b. *The Running Man*
   c. *Escape from New York*
   d. *The Matrix*

5. Who took over the role of Mad Max in 2015's *Fury Road*?

   a. Vin Diesel
   b. Dwayne Johnson
   c. Tom Hardy
   d. Hugh Jackman

6. To where is Arnold Schwarzenegger trying to gain entry when he utters the line "I'll be back" in *The Terminator*?

   a. An office block
   b. A high school

c. A police station

d. A bank

7. Which action star appeared in *Cliffhanger*, *Demolition Man*, and *The Specialist* in the 1990s?

   a. Arnold Schwarzenegger

   b. Sylvester Stallone

   c. Jean-Claude Van Damme

   d. Steven Seagal

8. What speed does the bus have to maintain in the 1994 action blockbuster of the same name starring Keanu Reeves and Sandra Bullock?

   a. 40 miles per hour

   b. 50 miles per hour

   c. 60 miles per hour

   d. 70 miles per hour

9. *Maverick* was the 2022 sequel to what 1980s blockbuster?

   a. *Top Gun*

   b. *Raw Deal*

   c. *Road House*

   d. *Tron*

10. Which American author wrote the series of novels on which the *Bourne* trilogy is based?

    a. Dan Brown

    b. Patrick Larkin

    c. Robert Ludlum

    d. Tom Clancy

11. True or False? Future Oscar-winner Michelle Yeoh was just 18 years old when she appeared in Ang Lee's *Crouching Tiger, Hidden Dragon* in 2000.

12. Who plays John Wick in the action movie series of the 2010s and 2020s?

    a. Keanu Reeves

    b. Nicholas Cage

    c. Tobey Maguire

    d. Andrew Garfield

13. The 2022 period action movie *Prey* was a critically acclaimed installment in what sci-fi action franchise?

    a. *Transformers*
    b. *The Matrix*
    c. *Predator*
    d. *Blade Runner*

14. By what nickname is Uma Thurman's character known in the *Kill Bill* movies?

    a. The Bride
    b. The Mother
    c. The Daughter
    d. The Teacher

15. Put these John Woo action blockbusters in chronological order, earliest first:

    a. *Mission: Impossible 2*
    b. *Face/Off*
    c. *The Killer*
    d. *Hard Target*

16. The band of robbers in 1991's *Point Break* disguise themselves using masks resembling what as they carry out their raids?

    a. Animals
    b. Monsters
    c. Presidents
    d. Superheroes

17. Which legendary action director's movies include *The Rock, Armageddon*, and the *Transformers* franchise?

    a. Tony Scott
    b. John McTiernan
    c. Paul Verhoeven
    d. Michael Bay

18. Who plays the estranged husband of Helen Hunt's storm-chasing meteorologist Jo in the 1996 action disaster movie *Twister*?

    a. Jeff Bridges
    b. Pierce Brosnan
    c. Bruce Willis
    d. Bill Paxton

ANSWERS

1. B. Olivia de Havilland. The movie also featured early Hollywood legends Basil Rathbone and Claude Rains as Guy of Gisbourne and Prince John, respectively.
2. B. *Die Hard*. The 34-story Fox Plaza (now 2121 Avenue of the Stars) actually stood in for the Nakatomi building in the movie.
3. C. 1930s. The movie is set in 1936.
4. D. *The Matrix*. An earlier idea of swallowing a red pill to see what the world is truly like had been featured in 1990's *Total Recall*, but it was *The Matrix* in 1999 that introduced the blue pill and established a trope that is still circulated today.
5. C. Tom Hardy. *Mad Max: Fury Road* had been in development since the late 1980s by the time Tom Hardy was cast in 2010. Other actors who had been considered for the part over the years included Jeremy Renner, Michael Fassbender, Eric Bana, and even Eminem.
6. C. A police station. The line has since been reused or played upon in all of the subsequent *Terminator* movies, albeit with variations along the way. Schwarzenegger's co-star, Linda Hamilton, gets to say it in 2019's *Dark Fate*, while the line is reworked as "She'll be back" in *Terminator 3: Rise of the Machines* in reference to the movie's robotic villainess, T-X (played by Kristanna Loken).
7. B. Sylvester Stallone. After his successes with both the *Rocky* and *Rambo* franchises in the 1970s and 80s, the 90s were when Sly truly stepped into his action hero phase with movies like these and *Daylight*, *Assassins*, and *Judge Dredd*.
8. B. 50 miles per hour. As part of the training for the movie, Sandra Bullock got an actual Santa Monica bus driver's license.
9. A. *Top Gun*. Arriving 36 years after the 1986 original, *Top Gun: Maverick* grossed just under $1.5 billion at the box office in 2022, making it one of the most successful movies of all time.
10. C. Robert Ludlum. After Ludlum's death in 2001, Eric Van Lustbader took over the reins of the Jason Bourne character, and he added a further 11 novels to the series. Since 2020, author Brian Freedman has taken over the franchise, and there are now more than 20 books in the entire series.
11. False. In fact, she was 38 when the film was released.
12. A. Keanu Reeves. The franchise has proved a global hit, with the first four movies in the series alone grossing over $1 billion worldwide.

13. C. *Predator. Prey* is set in 1719 and has the alien warrior from the long-running franchise battling against French voyageurs and native Comanche peoples.
14. A. The Bride. The character's real name is Beatrice Kiddo, and her codename in Bill's group of assassins is Black Mamba.
15. C. *The Killer* (1989), D. *Hard Target* (1993), B. *Face/Off* (1997), A. *Mission: Impossible 2* (2000).
16. C. Presidents. The robbers themselves are known as the Ex-Presidents in the movie and wear masks resembling presidents Ronald Reagan, Jimmy Carter, Richard Nixon, and Lyndon B. Johnson.
17. D. Michael Bay. Bay's movies also include the *Bad Boys* movies, *Pearl Harbor*, and *The Island*.
18. D. Bill Paxton. The role was reportedly offered to Tom Hanks originally, but he passed on it and suggested Paxton — who had worked with him on the previous year's *Apollo 13* — be cast instead.

DID YOU KNOW?

The very first action movie in film history is popularly said to be a silent epic, *The Great Train Robbery*, filmed in 1903!

CHAPTER 7
BLACK AND WHITE CLASSICS

There was no overnight switch from black and white to color movies, and they co-existed for decades as the two technologies continued to develop—with many directors still opting to make black and white movies today!

1. How old was Orson Welles when he wrote, directed, and starred in *Citizen Kane*?

    a. 25
    b. 35
    c. 45
    d. 55

2. True or False? In the scene in *The Wizard of Oz* where the action moves from black and white to Technicolor, an early green screen was used to superimpose the colorful world of Oz into the black and white background.

    e. Which of these Tim Burton movies is shot in black and white?
    f. *Edward Scissorhands*
    g. *Ed Wood*
    h. *The Corpse Bride*
    i. *Dark Shadows*

3. Who directed 1951's *Strangers on a Train*?

    a. Billy Wilder
    b. Cecil B. DeMille
    c. John Ford
    d. Alfred Hitchcock

4. Who starred in the comic movies *A Night at the Opera* and *A Day at the Races*?

    a. Charlie Chaplin
    b. Buster Keaton
    c. Laurel and Hardy
    d. The Marx Brothers

5. What 1944 thriller starred Fred MacCauley as an insurance representative coerced into fraud by a femme fatale, played by Barbara Stanwyck?

    a. *Suspicion*
    b. *Shadow of a Doubt*
    c. *Notorious*
    d. *Double Indemnity*

6. Who starred in the 1944 thriller *Gaslight*, from which the word *gaslighting* has since been coined?

   a. Vivien Leigh
   b. Ingrid Bergman
   c. Gloria Swanson
   d. Greta Garbo

7. What classic American novel was adapted for the big screen starring Henry Fonda in 1940?

   a. *The Grapes of Wrath*
   b. *East of Eden*
   c. *Cannery Row*
   d. *Of Mice and Men*

8. Who directed the 2021 black and white drama *Belfast*?

   a. Steven Spielberg
   b. David Fincher
   c. Kenneth Branagh
   d. Jane Campion

9. Put these black and white horrors in chronological order, earliest first:

   a. *The Haunting*
   b. *Night of the Living Dead*
   c. *Psycho*
   d. *Cat People*

10. In 2012, *The Artist* became the first black and white movie to win the Oscar for Best Picture in how many years?

    a. 19
    b. 39
    c. 59
    d. 79

11. Which of these festive classics is not a black and white movie?

    a. *It's A Wonderful Life*
    b. *Miracle on 34th Street (1947)*
    c. *White Christmas*
    d. *Holiday Inn*

12. A classic 1964 black and white thriller was entitled *Séance on a ...* what?

a. ... *Stormy Night*
b. ... *Sunday Morning*
c. ... *Wet Afternoon*
d. ... *Dark Weekend*

13. True or False? More black and white films have won the Best Picture Oscar than color films.

14. The 1964 black and white thriller *Hush...Hush, Sweet Charlotte* was meant to be the follow-up to what 1962 movie?

    a. *Whatever Happened to Baby Jane?*
    b. *Cape Fear*
    c. *Blow-Up*
    d. *The Manchurian Candidate*

15. What black and white classic was Alfred Hitchcock's first American movie?

    a. *Rebecca*
    b. *Psycho*
    c. *Spellbound*
    d. *Lifeboat*

16. The 1941 noir *The Maltese Falcon* was based on a book by which American author?

    a. Raymond Chandler
    b. Dashiell Hammett
    c. Henry James
    d. Ernest Hemingway

17. Who directed the 1930s classics *Mr. Deeds Goes to Town* and *You Can't Take It With You*?

    a. Frank Capra
    b. Victor Fleming
    c. William Wyler
    d. Mervyn LeRoy

ANSWERS

1. A. 25. Filming on *Citizen Kane* began just two months after Welles' 25th birthday, in the summer of 1940.
2. False. In fact, the effect was done entirely practically, with a body double for Judy Garland—dressed in monochrome clothing on a special monochrome set—seen opening the door, before Garland herself, in full-color clothing, steps through it.
3. B. *Ed Wood*. Burton's tribute to the eponymous cult director is entirely black and white (as was his 2012 animated movie *Frankenweenie*).
4. D. Alfred Hitchcock. As well as being made by one of the most acclaimed movie directors of all time, *Strangers on a Train* was based on a novel by Patricia Highsmith and co-adapted for the screen by the legendary writer Raymond Chandler.
5. D. The Marx Brothers. These were the first movies the Marx Brothers made with MGM Studios and their first after the departure of Zeppo Marx from the group in 1933 to work behind the scenes as a talent agent.
6. D. *Double Indemnity*. Directed by Billy Wilder, *Double Indemnity* was written by Raymond Chandler (who earned an Oscar nomination for his work).
7. B. Ingrid Bergman. Her performance as a woman manipulated by her husband to question her own sanity earned Bergman the first of her three Academy Awards.
8. A. *The Grapes of Wrath*. The novel had won the Pulitzer Prize just the previous year.
9. C. Kenneth Branagh. The movie was a semi-autobiographical account of a young boy's childhood in Northern Ireland at the beginning of The Troubles.
10. D. *Cat People* (1942), C. *Psycho* (1960), A. *The Haunting* (1963), B. *Night of the Living Dead* (1968).
11. A. 19. *Schindler's List* took the same prize in 1993, meaning there had been only a 19-year gap between black-and-white winners. *The Artist* was, however, the first French film to win Best Picture, the first wholly black and white movie since 1960 (as *Schindler's List* includes some brief color), and the first silent film to win since 1929!
12. C. *White Christmas*. This 1954 musical classic, starring Bing Crosby and Danny Kaye, took its name from Irving Berlin's song "White

Christmas," which had been written for the festive movie *Holiday Inn* in 1942.

13. C. ... *Wet Afternoon.* The film, which tells the story of a medium who arranges the kidnapping of a child so she can convince the authorities of her psychic abilities, starred Kim Stanley and Richard Attenborough.
14. False. In fact, since 1929, almost twice as many color films have won as black and white.
15. A. *Whatever Happened to Baby Jane?* Joan Crawford was again meant to star alongside Bette Davis in *Sweet Charlotte* but dropped out of the production and was replaced by Olivia de Havilland.
16. A. *Rebecca.* The 1940 movie won the Academy Award for Best Picture and earned Hitchcock his first Oscar nomination as Best Director.
17. B. Dashiell Hammett. The film starred Humphrey Bogart as private investigator Sam Spade.
18. A. Frank Capra. Both films won the Oscar for Best Director.

DID YOU KNOW?

The first color film to win Best Picture at the Oscars was *Gone with the Wind* in 1939.

CHAPTER 8
WORLD CINEMA

Cinema hasn't always been an English-language — or a Hollywood — affair, of course! From early black and white European movies to foreign language Oscar-winners and nominees, this chapter looks at the wide world of...world cinema!

1. In what European city is the quirky romance *Amélie*, starring Audrey Tautou, set?

    a. Brussels
    b. Paris
    c. Geneva
    d. Nice

2. Which Hollywood legend was the first actor to win an Oscar for a performance spoken entirely in a language other than English?

    a. Max von Sydow
    b. Catherine Deneuve
    c. Ingrid Bergman
    d. Sophia Loren

3. What 1960 Federico Fellini movie tells the story of a journalist seeking love and acceptance in the culture of Rome?

    a. *La Strada*
    b. *8 ½*
    c. *Nights of Cabiria*
    d. *La Dolce Vita*

4. In 2025, Fernanda Torres became only the second Brazilian actress in history to be nominated for the Academy Award for Best Actress. Who was the other?

    a. Her sister
    b. Her daughter
    c. Her mother
    d. Her grandmother

5. Japan's Studio Ghibli and filmmaker Hayao Miyazaki are best known for their work in what genre?

    a. Horror
    b. Musicals
    c. Animation
    d. Science fiction

6. *Wolf Warrior 2*, *The Wandering Earth*, and *Hi, Mom* are some of the most successful non-English language movies of the 21st century. In what country were they made?

   a. Russia
   b. India
   c. Mexico
   d. China

7. Who won an Oscar for her part-Spanish performance in Woody Allen's comedy *Vicky Christina Barcelona*?

   a. Penélope Cruz
   b. Salma Hayek
   c. Eva Mendes
   d. Ana de Armas

8. Telling the story of immigrants arriving in rural Arkansas in the 1980s, the acclaimed 2019 drama *Minari* is partly in what language?

   a. Thai
   b. Korean
   c. Japanese
   d. Malay

9. Where are the eyes of the grotesque monster The Pale Man in Guillermo del Toro's 2006 film *Pan's Labyrinth*?

   a. On the back of his head
   b. In his chest
   c. On the tip of his tongue
   d. On the palms of his hands

10. What kind of monsters terrorize a high-speed rail service in the acclaimed South Korean action horror *Train to Busan*?

    a. Werewolves
    b. Vampires
    c. Aliens
    d. Zombies

11. Put these classics of world cinema in chronological order, starting with the earliest released:

    a. *Das Boot*
    b. *Battleship Potemkin*
    c. *City of God*
    d. *Seven Samurai*

12. The classic historical masterpiece *The Seventh Seal* was made in which European country?

   a. Greece
   b. Sweden
   c. Italy
   d. Germany

13. Which 1964 Hollywood western, starring Paul Newman, was based on Akira Kurosawa's Japanese classic *Rashomon*?

   a. *The Outrage*
   b. *Hud*
   c. *Hombre*
   d. *The Left Handed Gun*

14. Which of these is not one of the famous *Three Colours* trilogy of movies by Polish director Krzysztof Kieślowski?

   a. Red
   b. Yellow
   c. Blue
   d. White

15. What genre of movie is the acclaimed Swedish film *Let the Right One In*?

   a. Horror
   b. Comedy
   c. Biopic
   d. Science fiction

16. The South Korean action movie *Oldboy* features a memorable two-and-a-half-minute single-shot fight scene set entirely…where?

   a. A corridor
   b. A staircase
   c. A rooftop
   d. Underwater

17. Who directed the 2001 Mexican coming of age drama *Y tu mamá también*?

   a. Guillermo del Toro
   b. Alejandro González Iñárritu
   c. Carlos Carrera
   d. Alfonso Cuarón

18. What is the English title of the acclaimed French crime thriller *La Haine*?

    a. The Heat
    b. The Head
    c. The Hate
    d. The Hand

ANSWERS

1. B. Paris. In fact, the movie is set almost entirely in the Bohemian Paris district of Montmartre.
2. D. Sophia Loren. Italian actress Anna Magnani had earlier won the same award for her performance in the 1951 film *The Rose Tattoo*, but her performance was partly in English.
3. D. *La Dolce Vita*. Also known by its English title *The Good Life*, *La Dolce Vita* was hugely successful on its release and has since come to be regarded as one of the greatest films ever made.
4. C. Her mother. Torres' mother Fernanda Montenegro was nominated for the same award for the 1998 drama *Central Station*. Fernanda was nominated for her performance as the activist Eunice Paiva in *I'm Still Here* — in which her mother also briefly appeared, playing Eunice as an older woman.
5. C. Animation. Miyazaki is the director of Studio Ghibli's *Princess Mononoke* (1997), *Spirited Away* (2001), and *Howl's Moving Castle* (2004), among many other acclaimed animations.
6. D. China. Despite being little known outside of China, all three of these movies earned more than half a billion dollars at the global box office.
7. A. Penélope Cruz. The movie also stars Cruz's husband, Javier Bardem.
8. B. Korean. *Minari* was nominated for six Academy Awards, with its star Youn Yuh-jung taking the Oscar for Supporting Actress.
9. D. On the palms of his hands. The Pale Man was played by the American actor Doug Jones, who learned his Spanish-language lines phonetically.
10. D. Zombies. A zombie apocalypse breaks out during the train's journey, with the movie focusing on the passengers' attempts to survive it.
11. B. *Battleship Potemkin* (1925), D. *Seven Samurai* (1954), A. *Das Boot* (1980), C. *City of God* (2002).
12. B. Sweden. Featuring a memorable scene in which a knight plays chess with Death, the movie was directed by Ingmar Bergman.
13. A. *The Outrage*. Kurosawa even received a screenplay credit for *The Outrage*, despite not being involved in its production.

14. B. Yellow. A coproduction between France and Poland, the *Three Colours* movies — *Blue* (1993), *White* (1994), and *Red* (1994) — are meant to represent the French flag.
15. A. Horror. *Let the Right One In* tells the story of a young boy who befriends a vampire.
16. A. A corridor. The shot took three days to prepare and needed 17 takes to perfect.
17. D. Alfonso Cuarón. *Y tu mamá también* earned Cuarón an Oscar nomination for Original Screenplay.
18. C. The Hate. The film's title comes from a memorable line in the movie, "*La haine attire la haine*," or "Hatred breeds hatred."

DID YOU KNOW?

For the first time since records began, China overtook America as the world's biggest cinema-going country in both 2020 and 2021.

CHAPTER 9
CLASSIC ROMANCE

From classic tearjerkers to romcoms, this next set of questions celebrates the more romantic side of the movies.

1. Where do the couple at the center of the classic romantic movie *Brief Encounter* meet?

   a. A school
   b. A newspaper kiosk
   c. A tearoom
   d. A train station

2. Who starred opposite Cary Grant in *An Affair to Remember*?

   a. Deborah Kerr
   b. Eve Marie Saint
   c. Janet Leigh
   d. Audrey Hepburn

3. Who falls in love with Kate Winslet, before trying to have all memory of her erased after they break up, in the quirky romantic fantasy *Eternal Sunshine of the Spotless Mind*?

   a. Ethan Hawke
   b. Jim Carrey
   c. Ewan McGregor
   d. Elijah Wood

4. Following *Before Sunrise* and *Before Sunset*, what is the title of the third movie in Richard Linklater's *Before* trilogy, starring Ethan Hawke and Julie Delpy?

   a. *Before Nightfall*
   b. *Before Moonlight*
   c. *Before Midnight*
   d. *Before Evening*

5. Who starred opposite Robert Redford in *The Way We Were*?

   a. Jane Fonda
   b. Barbra Streisand
   c. Julie Christie
   d. Diane Keaton

6. What 2004 romance, starring Ryan Gosling and Rachel McAdams, was adapted from a novel by Nicholas Sparks?

   a. *The Astronaut's Wife*
   b. *The Fault in Our Stars*

c. *The Best of Me*

d. *The Notebook*

7. From what classic 1980s romance does the line "Nobody puts Baby in a corner" come?

    a. *Dirty Dancing*
    b. *Roxanne*
    c. *When Harry Met Sally...*
    d. *An Officer and a Gentleman*

8. What is the name of Julia Roberts' character in *Pretty Woman*?

    a. Vera
    b. Vivian
    c. Veronica
    d. Verity

9. Who starred opposite Tom Hanks in 1993's *Sleepless in Seattle*?

    a. Nicole Kidman
    b. Daryl Hannah
    c. Meg Ryan
    d. Debra Winger

10. Who won an Oscar for her role as an actress who falls for William Shakespeare in *Shakespeare in Love*?

    a. Gwyneth Paltrow
    b. Renée Zellweger
    c. Catherine Zeta-Jones
    d. Emma Thompson

11. What 1954 Billy Wilder romance starred Audrey Hepburn as the daughter of a chauffeur, who falls for the wealthy sons of the family for whom her father is the driver?

    a. *Sabrina*
    b. *Roman Holiday*
    c. *Funny Face*
    d. *Charade*

12. Which acclaimed English actress played Katharine, the love interest of the English patient in the 1992 film of the same name?

    a. Juliet Stevenson
    b. Kristin Scott Thomas

c. Joely Richardson

d. Rachel Weisz

13. In James Cameron's *Titanic*, what is the name of Rose's snobbish fiancé, played by Billy Zane?

a. Chris

b. Cal

c. Chuck

d. Cobb

14. What Hollywood legend starred as Tolstoy's *Anna Karenina* in the acclaimed MGM adaptation in 1935?

a. Greta Garbo

b. Marlene Dietrich

c. Jean Harlow

d. Rita Hayworth

15. Which of these actors has not appeared in an adaptation of *A Star is Born*?

a. Bradley Cooper

b. Ryan O'Neal

c. James Mason

d. Kris Kristofferson

16. What is the name of the handsome swashbuckler whom Robin Wright's Buttercup falls for in *The Princess Bride*?

a. Riley

b. Priestley

c. Westley

d. Harley

17. True or False? Filming of the musical romance *Moulin Rouge!* in 2000 had to be delayed when Ewan McGregor fell during one of the musical numbers and broke his leg.

18. Who plays David, the prime minister who falls for one of the staff of 10 Downing Street in *Love Actually*?

a. Alan Rickman

b. Hugh Grant

c. Colin Firth

d. Eddie Redmayne

ANSWERS

1. D. A train station. Directed by David Lean, the 1945 classic *Brief Encounter* starred Celia Johnson and Trevor Howard, and it was based on a play by Noël Coward.
2. A. Deborah Kerr. *An Affair to Remember* was ranked fourth on the American Film Institute's 100 Passions list in 2002.
3. B. Jim Carrey. Taking its title from a poem by Alexander Pope, *Eternal Sunshine* was written by Charlie Kaufman.
4. C. *Before Midnight*. Filmed at nine-year intervals beginning in 1995, the *Before* trilogy charts two young lovers who meet and fall in love in Europe.
5. B. Barbra Streisand. Streisand also recorded the title track, written by Marvin Hamlisch, which won the 1974 Oscar for Best Song.
6. D. *The Notebook*. Sparks is also the author of the books *Message in a Bottle* and *A Walk to Remember*, both of which have also been adapted into films.
7. A. *Dirty Dancing*. In 2005, this line was listed 98th on the American Film Institute's list of 100 classic movie quotes.
8. B. Vivian. The eponymous *Pretty Woman*'s name in the movie is Vivian Ward.
9. C. Meg Ryan. The pair also teamed up five years later for another classic '90s romcom, *You've Got Mail*.
10. A. Gwyneth Paltrow. Directed by John Madden, *Shakespeare in Love* won seven Academy Awards in all, from a total of 13 nominations.
11. A. *Sabrina*. Hepburn's two love interests in the movie were memorably played by Humphrey Bogart and William Holden.
12. B. Kristin Scott Thomas. Both Scott Thomas and Ralph Fiennes, who played the patient Almásy, were nominated for Oscars for their performances.
13. B. Cal. Matthew McConnaughey was originally offered the role of Cal, before the part went to Billy Zane.
14. A. Greta Garbo. Garbo starred opposite an all-star cast, including Fredric March, Maureen O'Sullivan, Freddie Bartholomew, and Basil Rathbone.
15. B. Ryan O'Neal. O'Neal starred opposite Barbra Streisand in the 1972 comedy *What's Up, Doc?*, but it was Kris Kristofferson who played her love interest in the 1976 adaptation of *A Star is Born*. Bradley

Cooper played the same role in the 2018 version, while James Mason took the part in 1954.
16. C. Westley. Played by Cary Elwes, Westley is also the Dread Pirate Roberts in the movie.
17. False. Actually, it was the movie's other star, Nicole Kidman, whose injuries held up the shoot!
18. B. Hugh Grant. The woman whom David falls for was played by English television actress and singer Martine McCutcheon.

DID YOU KNOW?

The deli in *When Harry Met Sally* was Katz's Deli on East Houston Street in New York, which now has a plaque on the table at which Meg Ryan sits in the film.

CHAPTER 10
SONGS & SOUNDTRACKS

Whether it's the screeching score of *Psycho* or the lush romantic strings of *Out of Africa*, music has always gone hand in hand with what is on the big screen—which is precisely the subject of this next set of questions!

1. Stanley Kubrick's epic *2001: A Space Odyssey* used a famous piece of music by what German composer?

   a. J.S. Bach
   b. Ludwig van Beethoven
   c. Richard Strauss
   d. Felix Mendelssohn

2. What Oscar-winning song features the line "Away above the chimney tops / That's where you'll find me"?

   a. "Beauty and the Beast"
   b. "When You Wish Upon a Star"
   c. "Circle of Life"
   d. "Over the Rainbow"

3. Who composed the iconic soundtrack to Steven Spielberg's *Jaws*?

   a. Jerry Goldsmith
   b. Henry Mancini
   c. John Williams
   d. Alfred Newman

4. Which actress famously recorded the Oscar-winning title song from Disney's *Beauty and the Beast* in a single take?

   a. Angela Lansbury
   b. Bernadette Peters
   c. Julie Andrews
   d. Audra McDonald

5. Which Oscar-nominated composer is known for his frequent collaborations with Tim Burton and has written scores for the likes of *Edward Scissorhands*, *Mars Attacks!*, and *Sleepy Hollow*?

   a. John Williams
   b. Danny Elfman
   c. James Newton Howard
   d. James Horner

6. Which of these artists has not won the Academy Award for Best Original Song?

a. Bob Dylan
b. Eminem
c. Mary J. Blige
d. Bruce Springsteen

7. The electronic composer and musician Vangelis is best known for his famous score to what 1981 drama?

   a. *An Officer and a Gentleman*
   b. *Chariots of Fire*
   c. *Poltergeist*
   d. *Midnight Express*

8. Which of these epics movies was not scored by Hans Zimmer?

   a. *Gladiator*
   b. *Alien*
   c. *Inception*
   d. *Interstellar*

9. The lead vocalist of what classic American rock band has gone on to win two Oscars in the 21st century for his work on movie scores?

   a. Nine Inch Nails
   b. Green Day
   c. Aerosmith
   d. Pearl Jam

10. What Disney animation features the songs "How Far I'll Go" and "You're Welcome"?

    a. *Frozen*
    b. *Encanto*
    c. *Moana*
    d. *Tangled*

11. Scott Joplin's famous piano rag "The Entertainer" was used as the theme to what 1973 movie?

    a. *The Sting*
    b. *Smokey and the Bandit*
    c. *Every Which Way but Loose*
    d. *The Godfather*

12. Who made history in 1984 by simultaneously having America's number one film, number one album, and number one single, all for their work on the same movie?

a. Madonna
b. Barbra Streisand
c. Prince
d. Michael Jackson

13. Who scored the films *Field of Dreams, Braveheart, Titanic,* and *Avatar*?

    a. James Horner
    b. Ennio Morricone
    c. Maurice Jarre
    d. John Barry

14. Enya and Annie Lennox both contributed Oscar-nominated songs to the soundtracks of what 2000s movie series?

    a. *The Lord of the Rings*
    b. *Harry Potter*
    c. *James Bond*
    d. *The Dark Knight*

15. The composer Carter Burwell is known for his frequent collaborations with whom?

    a. Quentin Tarantino
    b. David Fincher
    c. Christopher Nolan
    d. The Coen Brothers

16. Which of these artists has won two Academy Awards for Best Original Song in the 2020s?

    a. Billie Eilish
    b. Adele
    c. Beyoncé
    d. Lady Gaga

17. Icelandic composer Hildur Guðnadóttir's Oscar-winning score to *Joker* is chiefly written for what instrument?

    a. Piano
    b. Cello
    c. Organ
    d. Clarinet

18. Put these iconic scores by John Williams in order, from earliest to most recent:

a. *Schindler's List*
b. *Harry Potter and the Sorcerer's Stone*
c. *Indiana Jones and the Temple of Doom*
d. *E.T. the Extra-Terrestrial*

ANSWERS

1. C. Richard Strauss. The opening fanfare or "Sunrise" of Richard Strauss' *Also sprach Zarathustra* was used as the movie's epic opening theme.
2. D. "Over the Rainbow." The song was almost cut from *The Wizard of Oz*, as several MGM executives argued that it was both too slow and too sad; it went on to win the 1939 Oscar for Best Original Song.
3. C. John Williams. Williams later described the famous score for *Jaws* as being as "instinctual, relentless, [and] unstoppable" as a shark attack.
4. A. Angela Lansbury. Lansbury — who voiced the teapot Mrs. Potts in *Beauty and the Beast* — was initially asked to record a test take by its songwriters, Alan Menken and Howard Ashman, but the recording was so good that it was included in the film.
5. B. Danny Elfman. Elfman also famously wrote the theme tunes to *The Simpsons* and *Desperate Housewives*.
6. C. Mary J. Blige. Mary J. Blige was nominated for the award for her work on the drama *Mudbound* in 2017 but lost out to "Remember Me" from Disney's *Coco*. Bob Dylan won for "Things Have Changed" from *Wonder Boys*, Eminem won for "Lose Yourself" from *8 Mile*, and Bruce Springsteen won for "Streets of Philadelphia" from the AIDS drama *Philadelphia*.
7. B. *Chariots of Fire*. Although also known for his work on the likes of *Blade Runner* and *Missing*, Vangelis' soundtrack to *Chariots of Fire* won him his only Oscar and Oscar nomination.
8. B. *Alien*. The original 1979 *Alien* movie was scored by Jerry Goldsmith.
9. A. Nine Inch Nails. Frontman Trent Reznor won the Best Original Score Oscars for both *The Social Network* and Pixar's *Soul*.
10. C. *Moana*. Like most of the songs from the movie, both were written by Lin-Manuel Miranda.
11. A. *The Sting*. In fact, several of Joplin's ragtime compositions were included in or adapted for the film by composer Marvin Hamlisch, including "Solace," "The Easy Winners," and "The Pineapple Rag."
12. C. Prince. Prince's movie *Purple Rain*, its soundtrack, and the song "When Doves Cry" taken from it, all held the top spot in 1984.
13. A. James Horner. Horner was nominated for an Academy Award for all four of these films, winning for *Titanic* in 1998.

14. A. *The Lord of the Rings*. Enya's track "May It Be" from *The Fellowship of the Ring* was nominated at the 2002 Oscars (losing out to Randy Newman's "If I Didn't Have You" from *Monsters, Inc.*), while Annie Lennox's "Into the West" was one of the 11 Academy Awards *The Return of the King* took home in its clean sweep two years later.
15. D. The Coen Brothers. To date, Burwell has scored all but two of the Coen Brothers' films, including *Miller's Crossing, Barton Fink, Fargo,* and *The Big Lebowski*.
16. A. Billie Eilish. To date, Beyoncé has been nominated for one Best Song Oscar, while Adele and Lady Gaga have each won one. Billie Eilish won twice in the 2020s, for the Bond theme "No Time to Die" and "What Was I Made For?" from *Barbie*.
17. B. Cello. Guðnadóttir is a cellist and used the instrument as the centerpiece of her critically acclaimed Oscar-winning *Joker* score.
18. D. E.T. the Extra-Terrestrial (1982), C. *Indiana Jones and the Temple of Doom* (1984), A. *Schindler's List* (1993), B. *Harry Potter and the Sorcerer's Stone* (2001).

DID YOU KNOW?

Originally, any song merely included in a film was eligible for the Best Song Oscar, but the rules were changed in 1941 after Jerome Kern's song "The Last Time I Saw Paris" won the award, despite Kern writing it years earlier. Now, any eligible song must be written specifically *for* a film released in the previous year.

CHAPTER 11
THE GOLDEN AGE
OF HOLLYWOOD

The Golden Age of Hollywood is the name given to the period in the 1930s, '40s, and '50s during which Los Angeles emerged as the center of global cinema, and the first true icons of movie acting became superstars worldwide.

1. In what classic 1950 movie did Bette Davis play aging Broadway actress Margo Channing?

    a. *Dark Victory*
    b. *Jezebel*
    c. *The Letter*
    d. *All About Eve*

2. What classic Golden Age drama was based on an earlier story called *Everybody Comes to Rick's*?

    a. *Hold Back the Dawn*
    b. *In Which We Serve*
    c. *Casablanca*
    d. *The Lost Weekend*

3. Who was the only one of the four stars of 1951's *A Streetcar Named Desire* who did not win an Oscar for their performance?

    a. Marlon Brando
    b. Vivien Leigh
    c. Karl Malden
    d. Kim Hunter

4. Director Sidney Lumet made his debut feature in 1957 with an Oscar-nominated legal drama that has since gone on to be considered one of the greatest films of all time. What was it?

    a. *Witness for the Prosecution*
    b. *12 Angry Men*
    c. *To Kill A Mockingbird*
    d. *Anatomy of a Murder*

5. What is "Baby" in the 1938 comedy *Bringing Up Baby*?

    a. Wolf
    b. Alligator
    c. Leopard
    d. Chimpanzee

6. The 1944 romance *To Have and Have Not* starred what legendary Hollywood couple?

   a. Tony Curtis and Janet Leigh
   b. Fred Astaire and Ginger Rogers
   c. Humphrey Bogart and Lauren Bacall
   d. Clark Gable and Carole Lombard

7. Which of the Marx Brothers never spoke?

   a. Groucho
   b. Chico
   c. Harpo
   d. Zeppo

8. Who directed Clark Gable and Claudette Colbert in the 1934 comedy *It Happened One Night*?

   a. John Ford
   b. Frank Capra
   c. William Wyler
   d. George Cukor

9. Put these classic 1940s movies in order, from earliest to latest:

   a. *How Green Was My Valley*
   b. *For Whom the Bell Tolls*
   c. *Sands of Iwo Jima*
   d. *Road to Rio*

10. Which actress, best known for a long-running role on 1960s television, played Orson Welles' mother in *Citizen Kane*?

    a. Agnes Moorehead
    b. Patty Duke
    c. Lucille Ball
    d. Julie Newmar

11. Who played the fading star Norma Desmond in Billy Wilder's classic noir *Sunset Boulevard*?

    a. Marlene Dietrich
    b. Nancy Carroll
    c. Marie Dressler
    d. Gloria Swanson

12. Which future Hollywood legend made his debut in *Rebel Without a Cause* at the age of just 19?

a. Clint Eastwood
b. Gene Hackman
c. Dennis Hopper
d. Sean Connery

13. Who directed 1959's *Some Like it Hot*?

a. Robert Wise
b. Vincente Minnelli
c. Billy Wilder
d. Sidney Lumet

14. In what 1951 movie did Katharine Hepburn play a character named Rose Sayer?

a. *The African Queen*
b. *Long Day's Journey Into Night*
c. *The Philadelphia Story*
d. *Bringing Up Baby*

15. Who starred alongside Frank Sinatra in the 1957 comedy musical *Pal Joey*?

a. Ginger Rogers
b. Rita Hayworth
c. Marilyn Monroe
d. Jean Arthur

16. Who wrote the novella on which Audrey Hepburn's *Breakfast at Tiffany's* was based?

a. J.D. Salinger
b. Truman Capote
c. F. Scott Fitzgerald
d. Sylvia Plath

17. True or False? Despite producing many of the biggest films of Hollywood's Golden Age, John Ford never won the Academy Award for Best Director.

18. Which of these Golden Age actors did not appear in *From Here to Eternity*?

a. Burt Lancaster
b. Rock Hudson
c. Frank Sinatra
d. Montgomery Clift

ANSWERS

1. D. *All About Eve*. Davis's performance earned the actress her eighth Oscar nomination.
2. C. *Casablanca*. *Everybody Comes to Rick's* was a stage play written by debut writers Murray Burnett and Joan Alison, which they sold to Warner Bros. for $20,000.
3. A. Marlon Brando. Leigh, Malden, and Hunter won the awards for Best Actress, Supporting Actor, and Supporting Actress, but Brando lost out in the Best Actor race to Humphrey Bogart in *The African Queen*.
4. B. *12 Angry Men*. Lumet was just 33 at the time.
5. C. Leopard. *Bringing Up Baby* was notoriously a box office bomb on its release, but it has since gone on to be considered one of the greatest screwball comedies of Hollywood's Golden Age.
6. C. Humphrey Bogart and Lauren Bacall. Bogey and Bacall starred in five movies together, of which this was the first.
7. D. Zeppo. The mute performances by Zeppo inspired Walt Disney's depiction of Dopey in *Snow White*.
8. C. Frank Capra. The movie earned Capra the first of his three Best Director Oscars.
9. A. *How Green Was My Valley* (1941), B. *For Whom the Bell Tolls* (1943), D. *Road to Rio* (1947), C. *Sands of Iwo Gima* (1949).
10. A. Agnes Moorehead. Moorehead is perhaps best-known today for her role as Endora in the ABC sitcom *Bewitched*.
11. D. Gloria Swanson. Swanson earned the third of her Best Actress Oscar nominations for her performance in the film.
12. C. Dennis Hopper. Hopper played Goon in 1955's *Rebel Without a Cause* and followed it up with a role in another James Dean movie, *Giant*, the next year.
13. C. Billy Wilder. The movie earned Wilder his record fifth Best Director Oscar nomination of the decade.
14. A. *The African Queen*. Hepburn was nominated for an Oscar for her performance, losing out to Vivien Leigh in *A Streetcar Named Desire*.
15. B. Rita Hayworth. The movie also starred Kim Novak and Barbara Nichols.
16. B. Truman Capote. Capote was reportedly unhappy with Audrey Hepburn being cast in the role of Holly Golightly, as he had envisaged Marilyn Monroe in the part.

17. False. In fact, Ford won four Best Director Oscars — for *The Informer* (1935), *The Grapes of Wrath* (1940), *How Green Was My Valley* (1941), and *The Quiet Man* (1952).
18. B. Rock Hudson. Lancaster, Sinatra, and Clift all starred in the movie alongside Deborah Kerr and Donna Reed.

DID YOU KNOW?

To cinema historians, Hollywood's Golden Age ended in the 1960s, when the more subversive age now known as New Hollywood took over.

CHAPTER 12
CHILD STARS

Some of the greatest performances in movie history have been the work of stars still young enough to attend school! Child stars and cinematic early bloomers are the subject of this next chapter.

1. Having signed to MGM three years earlier, how old was Judy Garland when she starred in *The Wizard of Oz*?

   a. Eight
   b. 11
   c. 16
   d. 20

2. Which Hollywood actress played Haley Joel Osment's mother in *The Sixth Sense*?

   a. Toni Collette
   b. Cameron Diaz
   c. Julia Roberts
   d. Cate Blanchett

3. Child actor Justin Henry starred in what critically acclaimed 1979 drama?

   a. *Fanny and Alexander*
   b. *The Last Picture Show*
   c. *All the President's Men*
   d. *Kramer vs. Kramer*

4. Actor Jack Wild was just 16 years old when he was nominated for the Academy Award for Best Supporting Actor in 1968, playing what Dickens character?

   a. The Artful Dodger
   b. Pip
   c. David Copperfield
   d. Tiny Tim

5. Drew Barrymore had her breakthrough role as a child in what Steven Spielberg movie?

   a. *Close Encounters of the Third Kind*
   b. *E.T. the Extra Terrestrial*
   c. *Jurassic Park*
   d. *Jaws*

6. Which child star was the first recipient of an honorary miniature Oscar in 1934?

    a. Judy Garland
    b. Mickey Rooney
    c. Shirley Temple
    d. Hayley Mills

7. Which future Oscar-winner starred in the first *Freaky Friday* movie when she was just 13 years old?

    a. Holly Hunter
    b. Susan Sarandon
    c. Jodie Foster
    d. Gwyneth Paltrow

8. Which legendary actress began her career as a child star, appearing in 1943's *Lassie Come Home* at the age of 11?

    a. Elizabeth Taylor
    b. Brigitte Bardot
    c. Jayne Mansfield
    d. Natalie Wood

9. Which of these actresses was just 13 when she received her first Oscar nomination?

    a. Jennifer Lawrence
    b. Keira Knightly
    c. Saoirse Ronan
    d. Kate Winslet

10. Which of these movies does not star Elle Fanning?

    a. *Super 8*
    b. *Daddy Day Care*
    c. *War of the Worlds*
    d. *Maleficent*

11. True or False? When she received an Oscar nomination for her role in *Beasts of the Southern Wind* in 2013, Quvenzhané Wallis became the first Oscar nominee to be born in the 21st century.

12. Which *Lord of the Rings* actor began his career as a child star, appearing in movies such as *Flipper*, *Deep Impact*, and *Forever Young* while still a teenager?

a. Orlando Bloom
b. Elijah Wood
c. Liv Tyler
d. Sean Astin

13. Which of these *Harry Potter* actors is the youngest?

    a. Daniel Radcliffe
    b. Rupert Grint
    c. Emma Watson
    d. Tom Felton

14. Which of these former child stars connects the movies *Sleepy Hollow*, *Monster*, and *The Ice Storm*?

    a. Christina Ricci
    b. Tatum O'Neal
    c. Freddie Highmore
    d. Mara Wilson

15. True or False? Leonardo DiCaprio was just 12 when he earned his first Oscar nomination.

16. Best known for his role in *Home Improvement*, television child star Jonathan Taylor Thomas partly provided the speaking voice for what 1990s Disney character?

    a. Aladdin
    b. Simba
    c. Hercules
    d. Tarzan

17. Chloë Grace Moretz was 15 when she starred in a 2013 remake of what Stephen King story?

    a. *Pet Sematary*
    b. *Salem's Lot*
    c. *Carrie*
    d. *It*

18. Which actress was just ten years old when she was cast opposite Brad Pitt and Tom Cruise in *Interview with the Vampire*?

    a. Anne Hathaway
    b. Jessica Biel
    c. Kirsten Dunst
    d. Anna Paquin

ANSWERS

1. C. 16. Garland signed with MGM Studios when she was just 13.
2. A. Toni Collette. Both she and Osment, who was just ten at the time, were nominated for Oscars for their performances.
3. D. *Kramer vs. Kramer*. Henry played Dustin Hoffman and Meryl Streep's child in the Oscar-winning drama.
4. A. The Artful Dodger. Wild was nominated for his performance in the movie musical *Oliver!*
5. B. *E.T. the Extra Terrestrial*. Barrymore was just seven years old when the movie was released in 1972.
6. C. Shirley Temple. All four of these actors have been presented with honorary Juvenile Oscars, but Temple's was the first.
7. C. Jodie Foster. Foster was an established Disney child star in the 1970s, appearing in the first *Freaky Friday* in 1976.
8. A. Elizabeth Taylor. Taylor's breakthrough role in *National Velvet* came soon after when she was just 12.
9. C. Saoirse Ronan. Ronan was nominated for her role in *Atonement* in 2008.
10. C. *War of the Worlds*. It was Elle's sister Dakota who appeared in Steven Spielberg's *War of the Worlds* in 2005.
11. True. Wallis was born in 2003 and was just nine when she received her Best Actress nomination.
12. B. Elijah Wood. In fact, Wood made his film debut in *Back to the Future Part II* (1989) at age eight.
13. C. Emma Watson. Watson was born in 1990, Daniel Radcliffe in 1989, Rupert Grint in 1988, and Tom Felton in 1987.
14. A. Christina Ricci. Best known for playing Wednesday in the *Addams Family* movies, Ricci made her screen debut in *Mermaids* at the age of nine.
15. False. DiCaprio began acting in his teens, but he was 19 by the time he was nominated for his performance in 1993's *What's Eating Gilbert Grape*.
16. B. Simba. Thomas provided the voice for young Simba in *The Lion King*, while Matthew Broderick voiced the adult Simba.
17. C. *Carrie*. Moretz took over the eponymous role of the troubled young girl from Sissy Spacek in the original 1976 movie.
18. C. Kirsten Dunst. Like Anna Paquin (who won an Oscar for her role in *The Piano* at age 11), Dunst was a child star who appeared in a

string of 1990s blockbusters, including *Interview with the Vampire*, *Little Women*, and *Jumanji*.

DID YOU KNOW?

Justin Henry (see question 3 here!) remains the youngest Oscar-nominee in the Academy's history, nominated for the Supporting Actor award at the age of just eight.

CHAPTER 13
ALFRED HITCHCOCK

Widely considered one of the greatest filmmakers of all time — and certainly one of the most influential — Sir Alfred Hitchcock's movies span an incredible six decades.

1. Who plays the first on-screen murder victim in *Psycho*?

    a. Tippi Hedren
    b. Janet Leigh
    c. Eve Marie Saint
    d. Grace Kelly

2. Much of which classic Hitchcock thriller is shot in real time?

    a. *Rope*
    b. *Strangers on a Train*
    c. *The Birds*
    d. *Foreign Correspondent*

3. Who played the suspected murderer spotted by James Stewart from his *Rear Window*?

    a. Gene Kelly
    b. Raymond Burr
    c. Clark Gable
    d. Burl Ives

4. Put these lesser-known Hitchcock movies in chronological order, earliest first:

    a. *Family Plot*
    b. *Shadow of a Doubt*
    c. *Jamaica Inn*
    d. *Topaz*

5. Alfred Hitchcock's 1950 thriller *Stage Fright* is notable in that it stars whom?

    a. His wife
    b. His daughter
    c. His mother
    d. His sister

6. Which of his films did Hitchcock adapt for cinema twice, in 1934 and 1956?

    a. *Murder!*
    b. *The Man Who Knew Too Much*

    c. *To Catch a Thief*

    d. *Frenzy*

7. With which composer did Hitchcock collaborate for the soundtracks to many of his films?

    a. John Barry

    b. Bernard Hermann

    c. Jerry Goldsmith

    d. Henry Mancini

8. Hitchcock's 1959 thriller *North by Northwest* features a famous scene on what monument?

    a. Eiffel Tower

    b. Statue of Liberty

    c. Big Ben clocktower

    d. Mount Rushmore

9. True or False? Hitchcock's biggest box office success was *Psycho*.

10. Which of these Hitchcock movies did not star Grace Kelly?

    a. *Dial M for Murder*

    b. *Rear Window*

    c. *The Catch a Thief*

    d. *Vertigo*

11. Which of these is not the site of an attack by *The Birds* in Hitchcock's gruesome thriller?

    a. An attic

    b. A school

    c. A jailhouse

    d. A phone booth

12. Which of these Hitchcock movies was released in the 1930s?

    a. *The 39 Steps*

    b. *The Paradine Case*

    c. *Spellbound*

    d. *Lifeboat*

13. Who starred opposite Cary Grant in the 1946 spy thriller *Notorious*?

    a. Gene Tierney

    b. Lauren Bacall

    c. Joan Blondell

    d. Ingrid Bergman

14. Which of these Hollywood legends never appeared in a Hitchcock movie?

   a. Julie Andrews
   b. Elizabeth Taylor
   c. Doris Day
   d. Tallulah Bankhead

15. Which Hollywood star was the only actor to win an Oscar for their performance in a Hitchcock movie?

   a. Laurence Olivier
   b. James Stewart
   c. Joan Fontaine
   d. Grace Kelly

16. True or False? The blood seen washing down the plughole in *Psycho* is real pigs' blood Hitchcock's production team sourced from a local butcher in Los Angeles.

17. Who made her film debut in Hitchcock's 1955 black comedy *The Trouble with Harry*?

   a. Goldie Hawn
   b. Olivia de Haviland
   c. Shirley MacLaine
   d. Olympia Dukakis

18. Hitchcock famously appeared as an extra in many of his movies — but in which of his films did he have a cameo role walking his own two pet dogs, Sealyham terriers Geoffrey and Stanley?

   a. *The Birds*
   b. *The 39 Steps*
   c. *Rear Window*
   d. *Saboteur*

ANSWERS

1. B. Janet Leigh. All four of these actresses starred in Hitchcock movies, but it was Janet Leigh, as Marion Crane, who was famously murdered in the shower in the opening act of *Psycho*.
2. A. *Rope*. Starring James Stewart as a man who hosts a party with a dead body in his apartment, Rope runs in real time over its 80-minute running time.
3. B. Raymond Burr. Despite a long career in Hollywood, Burr is best known for his role as television lawyer Perry Mason.
4. C. *Jamaica Inn* (1939), B. *Shadow of a Doubt* (1943), D. *Topaz* (1969), A. *Family Plot* (1976).
5. B. His daughter. Actress Patricia Hitchcock, known as Pat, made her debut in *Stage Fright* in 1950 before going on to appear in several more of her father's films.
6. B. *The Man Who Knew Too Much*. Hitchcock remade his earlier version of the film to end his contract with Paramount Pictures.
7. B. Bernard Hermann. It was he who wrote the famous string section for the shower attack in *Psycho*, as well as the scores for *Vertigo* and *North by Northwest*, among many other classics.
8. D. Mount Rushmore. Hitchcock was not permitted to film on Mount Rushmore, however, so real-life footage had to be spliced into a studio mock-up.
9. True. Despite the controversy that surrounded it, *Psycho* earned over $30 million at the box office.
10. D. *Vertigo*. It was Kim Novak who took on the role of the classic Hitchcock blonde in 1958's *Vertigo*.
11. C. A jailhouse. During the memorable attic attack scene, actress Tippi Hedren received a gash to her eye when a live gull was thrown at her.
12. A. *The 39 Steps*. *The 39 Steps* was released in 1935; all the other movies here were released in the 1940s.
13. D. Ingrid Bergman. The movie also starred Claude Rains, who was nominated for a Best Supporting Actor Oscar for his performance.
14. B. Elizabeth Taylor. Julie Andrews appeared in *Torn Curtain*, Doris Day in *The Man Who Knew Too Much*, and Tallulah Bankhead in *Lifeboat*.
15. C. Joan Fontaine. Both Joan Fontaine and Laurence Olivier were nominated for Academy Awards for their performances in *Rebecca*, but it was for 1941's *Suspicion* that Fontaine took home an Oscar.

16. False. In fact, the "blood" was Hershey's chocolate syrup!
17. C. Shirley MacLaine. She was just 21 at the time.
18. A. *The Birds*. Hitchcock is seen leaving a pet shop with his two pet dogs as Tippi Hedren walks by.

DID YOU KNOW?

When plans to use mechanical birds proved impossible, more than 25,000 live birds were captured in the wild to be used in the making of Hitchcock's *The Birds*.

CHAPTER 14
WESTERNS

One of Hollywood's most enduringly popular genres of film is the Western, which has been a mainstay of the cinema since the silent era. This next set of questions heads out West.

1. True or False? Despite being known as The Man with No Name, Clint Eastwood's character in Sergio Leone's iconic Westerns is named in several of the movies.

2. Which of these is the title of a film award once given to those who have made great contributions to the Western genre?
   a. Silver Lasso
   b. Golden Boot
   c. Bronze Horse
   d. Iron Hat

3. In what classic John Ford Western did John Wayne play a character named Ethan Edwards?
   a. *The Searchers*
   b. *The Sun Shines Bright*
   c. *The Horse Soldiers*
   d. *Fort Apache*

4. What '90s Western swept the boards at the 1991 Academy Awards, winning a total of seven Oscars from 12 nominations?
   a. *Tombstone*
   b. *Unforgiven*
   c. *Dances With Wolves*
   d. *The Quick and the Dead*

5. Which composer is well known for his work in the Western genre, with his score for *Once Upon a Time in the West* being one of the best-selling musical scores of all time?
   a. Jerome Moross
   b. Ennio Morricone
   c. Max Steiner
   d. Dimitri Tiomkin

6. Who played Henry, the Ringo Kid, in *Stagecoach*?
   a. John Wayne
   b. Charles Bronson
   c. Randolph Scott
   d. Lee Van Cleef

7. Who starred opposite Warren Beatty in Robert Altman's 1971 Western *McCabe & Mrs. Miller*?

    a. Jane Fonda
    b. Julie Christie
    c. Britt Ekland
    d. Farrah Fawcett

8. True or False? After Western epic *Cimarron* won the Best Picture Oscar in 1931, a Western wouldn't win the award again for another 30 years.

9. Which member of the Rat Pack starred alongside John Wayne in the Howard Hawks Western *Rio Bravo*?

    a. Frank Sinatra
    b. Dean Martin
    c. Mickey Rooney
    d. Joey Bishop

10. Put these classic Westerns in chronological order, from earliest first:

    a. *Vera Cruz*
    b. *Dodge City*
    c. *She Wore a Yellow Ribbon*
    d. *Butch Cassidy and the Sundance Kid*

11. Who starred in the title role in *Shane*?

    a. Clint Eastwood
    b. Audie Murphy
    c. Robert Mitchum
    d. Alan Ladd

12. Which famous figure from the Wild West did Brad Pitt play on the big screen in 2007?

    a. Billy the Kid
    b. Doc Holliday
    c. Jesse James
    d. Wild Bill Hickok

13. Which of these 1950s Westerns was remade in 2007, starring Russell Crowe?

    a. *3:10 to Yuma*
    b. *High Noon*

c. *Forty Guns*

d. *Johnny Guitar*

14. What classic Western musical was based on an earlier 1931 play called *Green Grow the Lilacs*?

    a. *Annie Get Your Gun*

    b. *Calamity Jane*

    c. *Oklahoma!*

    d. *A Ticket to Tomahawk*

15. Which Hollywood director claimed to have heard the story of his Wyatt Earp Western *My Darling Clementine* from Earp himself?

    a. Howard Hawks

    b. John Ford

    c. David Butler

    d. Sam Peckinpah

16. Who starred in the infamous 1969 Western *The Wild Bunch*?

    a. William Holden

    b. James Stewart

    c. Gary Cooper

    d. Marlon Brando

17. True or False? John Wayne made over 80 Westerns in his career.

18. Who remade the classic Western tale *True Grit* in 2010?

    a. Steven Spielberg

    b. The Coen Brothers

    c. Darren Aronofsky

    d. Ang Lee

ANSWERS

1. True. Although the character is anonymous, in Sergio Leone's *Dollars Trilogy* of spaghetti westerns, he is variously referred to as Joe, Manco, and Blondie.
2. B. Golden Boot. First awarded in 1983, past winners include Lee Van Kleef, Gene Autry, Red Buttons, and Jane Russell.
3. A. *The Searchers*. Often lauded as one of the greatest Westerns of all time, *The Searchers* opened to rave reviews in 1956.
4. C. *Dances with Wolves*. Despite running to just over three hours — and being mostly spoken in Lakota with English subtitles — *Dances with Wolves* was a commercial and critical blockbuster, taking over $450 million at the box office.
5. B. Ennio Morricone. Morricone scored eight Sergio Leone movies over 20 years of collaborations.
6. A. John Wayne. 1939's *Stagecoach* was John Wayne's breakthrough role, as before then he had mainly been a B-movie actor with little other on-screen experience.
7. B. Julie Christie. Altman labeled his movie an "anti-Western" because it went against many of the established tropes of the Western genre.
8. False. In fact, it would be 60 years (until *Dances with Wolves* in 1991).
9. B. Dean Martin. Martin played the town drunk, known only as "Dude" in the movie.
10. B. *Dodge City* (1939), C. *She Wore A Yellow Ribbon* (1949), A. *Vera Cruz* (1954), D. *Butch Cassidy and the Sundance Kid* (1969).
11. D. Alan Ladd. Ladd was arguably not a natural choice for a Western, as he disliked guns and was not good with them; a memorable scene in the 1953 classic *Shane* in which he has to demonstrate his skills took 116 takes!
12. C. Jesse James. Pitt starred opposite Casey Affleck in Andrew Dominik's *The Assassination of Jesse James by the Coward Robert Ford*.
13. A. *3:10 to Yuma*. The 2007 movie also starred Christian Bale and Peter Fonda.
14. C. *Oklahoma!* Rodgers and Hammerstein's *Oklahoma!* debuted on Broadway in 1943, before being adapted for the big screen in 1955.
15. B. John Ford. *My Darling Clementine* told the story of the leadup to the OK Corral — a tale Ford had reportedly heard from Earp while working as a prop boy.

16. A. William Holden. *The Wild Bunch*, which also starred Ernest Borgnine and Robert Ryan, is now considered one of the greatest Westerns of all time.
17. True. In fact, Wayne made at least 83 appearances in Western movies throughout his career.
18. B. The Coen Brothers. The movie was nominated for ten Academy Awards but won zero.

DID YOU KNOW?

John Wayne's real name was Marion Mitchell Morrison.

CHAPTER 15
BIOPICS

A popular subject of the movies has always been the true-life story, with everyone from Elizabeth I to Elton John receiving the big-screen biopic treatment over the decades!

1. Who directed the 1962 epic *Lawrence of Arabia*?

    a. David Lean
    b. John Ford
    c. Robert Wise
    d. Elia Kazan

2. Which famous American figure did Leonardo DiCaprio play in Martin Scorsese's *The Aviator*?

    a. Andrew Carnegie
    b. Howard Hughes
    c. Henry Ford
    d. Charles Lindbergh

3. Put these 1980s biopics in the order of the era in which they are set, starting with the furthest back in time:

    a. *Amadeus*
    b. *Raging Bull*
    c. *The Elephant Man*
    d. *The Last Emperor*

4. Who played *Malcolm X* in Spike Lee's 1985 biopic?

    a. Jamie Foxx
    b. Eddie Murphy
    c. Denzel Washington
    d. Morgan Freeman

5. Which king is the subject of the Oscar-winning 2010 biopic *The King's Speech*?

    a. Edward VIII
    b. George VI
    c. George V
    d. Edward VI

6. Which acclaimed French actress starred alongside Mel Gibson in the 1995 historical biopic *Braveheart*?

    a. Audrey Tautou
    b. Juliette Binoche

    c. Catherine Deneuve

    d. Sophie Marceau

7. Which actress earned her first Oscar nomination for playing Elizabeth I and won her first Oscar for playing Katharine Hepburn?

    a. Glenda Jackson

    b. Cate Blanchett

    c. Miranda Richardson

    d. Judi Dench

8. Who played Shakespeare in *Shakespeare in Love*?

    a. Joseph Fiennes

    b. Colin Farrell

    c. Colin Firth

    d. Jude Law

9. Biopics of all four of these famous figures have won the Academy Award for Best Actor in the 21st century. Put them in chronological order, oldest first:

    a. Ray Charles

    b. Freddie Mercury

    c. J. Robert Oppenheimer

    d. Abraham Lincoln

10. Whom did Monica Barbaro play opposite Timothée Chalamet in Bob Dylan's 2024 biopic *A Complete Unknown*?

    a. Joan Baez

    b. Joni Mitchell

    c. Carol King

    d. Karen Carpenter

11. Who directed Austin Butler in the 2022 biopic *Elvis*?

    a. Steven Spielberg

    b. Baz Luhrman

    c. Paul Thomas Anderson

    d. Todd Field

12. Who played June Carter Cash in 2005's *Walk the Line*?

    a. Reese Witherspoon

    b. Julia Roberts

    c. Michelle Pfeiffer

    d. Jennifer Connelly

13. Who did Jesse Eisenberg play in 2010's *The Social Network*?

    a. Mark Zuckerburg
    b. Sergey Brin
    c. Jack Dorsey
    d. Elon Musk

14. Which American author has been played on the big screen by Philip Seymour Hoffman and Toby Jones and on television by Tom Hollander?

    a. J.D. Salinger
    b. Mark Twain
    c. Edgar Allen Poe
    d. Truman Capote

15. True or False? Julianne Moore won an Oscar for playing Virginia Woolf in the 2002 drama *The Hours*.

    e. Who did Gary Oldman portray in Oliver Stone's acclaimed 1990 biopic *JFK*?
    f. Lyndon B. Johnson
    g. Earl Warren
    h. Jack Ruby
    i. Lee Harvey Oswald

16. The 2016 biographical drama *Hidden Figures* told the story of three female African-American mathematicians working at what organization in the early 1960s?

    a. FBI
    b. Harvard
    c. NASA
    d. The Pentagon

17. Which American singer did Sissy Spacek play in the 1980 biopic *Coal Miner's Daughter*?

    a. Emmylou Harris
    b. Dolly Parton
    c. Carly Simon
    d. Loretta Lynn

ANSWERS

1. A. David Lean. The epic movie, which runs almost four hours, earned Lean his second Best Director Oscar.
2. B. Howard Hughes. DiCaprio was nominated for an Oscar for his performance, while the movie itself picked up 11 nominations in total.
3. A. *Amadeus* (a retelling of the life of Mozart, set in the late 1700s), C. *The Elephant Man* (the life of John Merrick, set in the late 1800s), D. *The Last Emperor* (a biography of the final monarch of China's Qing dynasty, set in the early 1900s), B. *Raging Bull* (the life of boxer Jake LaMotta, set in the 1940s and '50s).
4. C. Denzel Washington. Washington was nominated for an Oscar for his performance.
5. B. George VI. Played by Colin Firth, who won an Oscar for the role.
6. D. Sophie Marceau. Marceau played the French princess Isabelle.
7. B. Cate Blanchett. All four of those acclaimed actresses have memorably played Elizabeth I, but Blanchett was nominated for her role in *Elizabeth* in 1998 and then won for her role as Katharine Hepburn in *The Aviator* in 2004.
8. A. Joseph Fiennes. Although not a true biopic of William Shakespeare himself, 1998's *Shakespeare in Love* nevertheless kept many of the details of the Bard's life in the movie.
9. A. Ray Charles (won by Jamie Foxx in *Ray* in 2004), D. Abraham Lincoln (Daniel Day-Lewis in *Lincoln*, 2012), B. Freddie Mercury (Remi Malik in *Bohemian Rhapsody*, 2018), C. J. Robert Oppenheimer (Cillian Murphy in *Oppenheimer*, 2023).
10. A. Joan Baez. Barbaro was nominated for an Oscar for her performance, as was Chalamet.
11. B. Baz Luhrman. Although the movie was nominated for Best Picture at the 2023 Oscars, Luhrman was not nominated as Best Director.
12. A. Reese Witherspoon. The movie also starred Joaquin Phoenix as Johnny Cash.
13. A. Mark Zuckerburg. The movie also starred Andrew Garfield as Facebook co-founder Eduardo Saverin and Justin Timberlake as Napster founder Sean Parker.
14. D. Truman Capote. Hoffman won an Oscar for his performance in *Capote*, Toby Jones played him a year later in *Infamous*, and Tom

Hollander played him in the Hulu series *Feud: Capote vs. The Swans* in 2024.

15. False. Moore was in the movie (and was nominated for an Oscar), but it was Nicole Kidman who won the Oscar as Virginia Woolf.
16. D. Lee Harvey Oswald. Oswald's killer Jack Ruby was played by Brian Doyle-Murray.
17. C. NASA. The movie dramatized the work of Katherine Goble Johnson (Taraji P. Henson), Dorothy Vaughan (Octavia Spencer), and Mary Jackson (Janelle Monáe) in NASA's Space Race program.
18. D. Loretta Lynn. The film charted country music legend Loretta Lynn's early life, including her marriage at just 15 years of age.

DID YOU KNOW?

The first biopic in history is said to be Georges Méliès' 1900 silent *Joan of Arc*, though Thomas Edison had earlier produced *The Execution of Mary Stuart* in 1895 — but it had a run time of just 18 seconds!

CHAPTER 16
CLASSIC DRAMAS

Whether based in real life or not, drama is at the crux of all movie storytelling—with some of cinema's greatest dramas featuring in this next set of questions.

1. True or False? Movie censors originally demanded that the word "damn" in Rhett Butler's famous final line in *Gone with the Wind*—"Frankly, my dear, I don't give a damn"—be muted, and the movie was released to theaters with the audio cut for the split-second the word is spoken.

2. Alfred Hitchcock's 1966 thriller *Torn Curtain* is set during what era?
   a. The Cold War
   b. Prohibition Era
   c. World War II
   d. Industrial Revolution

3. Which comic actor starred as a jeweler in the 2019 drama *Uncut Gems*?
   a. Mike Myers
   b. Dana Carvey
   c. Rob Schneider
   d. Adam Sandler

4. Put these breakup and divorce dramas in order, oldest to most recent:
   a. *Marriage Story*
   b. *Stepmom*
   c. *Kramer vs. Kramer*
   d. *Boyhood*

5. True or False? The 2002 drama *The Hours* was based in part on Virginia Woolf's novel *To the Lighthouse*.
   a. Who won an Oscar for her performance as *Mrs. Miniver* in 1942?
   a. Ingrid Bergman
   b. Greer Garson
   c. Joan Blondell
   d. Veronica Lake

6. In what country is 2003's *Lost in Translation* set?
   a. Italy
   b. China
   c. Japan
   d. Iceland

7. Who starred in 1999's trans drama *Boys Don't Cry*?

    a. Jodie Foster
    b. Geena Davis
    c. Holly Hunter
    d. Hilary Swank

8. In what US state does 1967's race drama *In the Heat of the Night* take place?

    a. Mississippi
    b. Alabama
    c. Florida
    d. Utah

9. Who played small-time criminal hustler J.D. in *Thelma & Louise*?

    a. George Clooney
    b. Brad Pitt
    c. Grant Show
    d. Mark Ruffalo

10. Which legendary director made the 1950s dramas *Witness for the Prosecution*, *Stalag 17*, and *Sunset Boulevard*?

    a. Billy Wilder
    b. Joseph L. Mankiewicz
    c. John Huston
    d. Carol Reed

11. Who played the title role in Roman Polanski's war drama *The Pianist*?

    a. Liam Neeson
    b. Adrian Brody
    c. Jack Nicholson
    d. Robert Downey, Jr.

12. Which of these Hollywood legends did not star in the classic 1959 drama *Suddenly, Last Summer*?

    a. Elizabeth Taylor
    b. Audrey Hepburn
    c. Montgomery Clift
    d. Katharine Hepburn

13. Where are the dramas *One Flew Over the Cuckoo's Nest*, *Awakenings*, and *Girl, Interrupted* set?

a. Psychiatric hospitals
b. Military barracks
c. High schools
d. Hotels

14. Which acclaimed British actress starred opposite Cate Blanchett as a deranged schoolteacher in *Notes on a Scandal*?

a. Maggie Smith
b. Judi Dench
c. Vanessa Redgrave
d. Helen Mirren

15. Which British actor won a record three consecutive Supporting Actor BAFTAs in the 1980s for his roles in *Trading Places, A Private Function*, and the political drama *Defence of the Realm*?

a. Ian Holm
b. Denholm Elliott
c. Bob Hoskins
d. Robbie Coltrane

16. Put these 1960s, '70s, and '80s Best Picture Oscar-winning dramas in order, starting with the earliest released:

a. *The Deer Hunter*
b. *Patton*
c. *Out of Africa*
d. *Midnight Cowboy*

17. True or False? No actor has ever won an Oscar for playing Hamlet.

ANSWERS

1. False. Although a popular movie myth claims David O. Selznick was fined for including "damn" in the film, censorship of curse words had been relaxed just months before its release, allowing the line to go unedited.
2. A. The Cold War. The movie tells the story of an American nuclear scientist, played by Paul Newman, who appears to defect to East Germany.
3. D. Adam Sandler. The movie tells the story of a jeweler who needs to track down a gemstone in order to pay off his gambling debts.
4. C. *Kramer vs. Kramer* (1979), B. *Stepmom* (1998), D. *Boyhood* (2014), A. *Marriage Story* (2010).
5. False. It partly dramatized Woolf's novel *Mrs. Dalloway*.
6. B. Greer Garson. The movie was the first Oscar winner to chart the realities of World War II.
7. C. Japan. The film follows two out-of-place characters as they struggle to fit in in Tokyo.
8. D. Hilary Swank. The movie told the story of a trans man trying to find a new life for himself in Nebraska.
9. A. Mississippi. The movie starred Sidney Poitier as a Philadelphia cop brought to Mississippi to investigate a murder.
10. B. Brad Pitt. During casting, *Thelma & Louise* star Geena Davis did screen tests with all four of these actors but recommended Pitt for the role.
11. A. Billy Wilder. Wilder also wrote or co-wrote the screenplays for all three movies, winning the Oscar for his script for *Sunset Boulevard*.
12. B. Adrian Brody. Brody won his first Best Actor Oscar for his role as the Polish-Jewish pianist and Holocaust survivor Władysław Szpilman.
13. B. Audrey Hepburn. The movie told the story of a young, mentally disturbed woman, Elizabeth Taylor, and the wealthy aunt overseeing her care, Katharine Hepburn.
14. A. Psychiatric hospitals. *One Flew Over the Cuckoo's Nest* famously swept the boards at the 1976 Oscars, while Robin Williams' *Awakenings* was nominated for three in 1991, and Angelina Jolie won Supporting Actress for her role in *Girl, Interrupted* in 2000.
15. B. Judi Dench. The movie was based on the novel of the same title by Zoë Heller.

16. Denholm Elliott. Best known for his role in the *Indiana Jones* movies, Elliott won three consecutive BAFTAs in 1983, 1984, and 1985.
17. D. *Midnight Cowboy* (1969), B. *Patton* (1970), A. *The Deer Hunter* (1978), C. *Out of Africa* (1985).
18. False. Laurence Olivier won the 1948 award for his portrayal of Hamlet, which also won that year's Best Picture award.

DID YOU KNOW?

In the American Film Institute's 100 Years poll, Orson Welles' drama *Citizen Kane* was named the best film of all time, while *Casablanca* was named the best romance and *To Kill a Mockingbird* the best courtroom drama.

CHAPTER 17
FANTASY EPICS

Movies don't just reflect real life; they take us to wholly invented fantasy worlds, too. The escapist fantasy epics of the last 100 years of cinema are the subject of these next questions.

1. Who plays Saruman in Peter Jackson's *Lord of the Rings* and *Hobbit* trilogies?

   a. Ian Holm
   b. Christopher Lee
   c. Derek Jacobi
   d. John Hurt

2. In the *Harry Potter* movies, what kind of creature is Firenze?

   a. Centaur
   b. Spider
   c. Unicorn
   d. Troll

3. The 1985 fantasy *Legend* was an early film starring which actor?

   a. Val Kilmer
   b. Mel Gibson
   c. Richard Gere
   d. Tom Cruise

4. Put these 1980s fantasy epics in order, starting with the earliest released:

   a. *Willow*
   b. *Conan the Barbarian*
   c. *Highlander*
   d. *The Neverending Story*

5. Which of these comic actors did not appear in 1987's *The Princess Bride*?

   a. Billy Crystal
   b. Peter Cook
   c. Mel Brooks
   d. Christopher Guest

6. True or False? The theatrical runtime of Peter Jackson's three *Hobbit* movies is longer than the runtime of the original theatrical release of the *Lord of the Rings* movies.

7. Who directed a 2009 big-screen adaptation of the classic children's story *Where the Wild Things Are*?

   a. Wes Anderson
   b. Spike Jonze
   c. Tim Burton
   d. Guillermo del Toro

8. Who played the faun Mr. Tumnus in the live-action *Chronicles of Narnia* movies?

   a. James McAvoy
   b. Liam Neeson
   c. Rupert Everett
   d. Ray Winstone

9. Who played a witch in the 2007 fantasy movie *Stardust*?

   a. Susan Sarandon
   b. Meryl Streep
   c. Michelle Pfeiffer
   d. Geena Davis

10. Who did Laurence Olivier play in the 1981 mythological fantasy *Clash of the Titans*?

   a. Achilles
   b. Zeus
   c. Hades
   d. Poseidon

11. Who directed the 1980s fantasies *Time Bandits* and *Brazil*?

   a. Wolfgang Petersen
   b. Terry Gilliam
   c. Ron Howard
   d. Desmond Davis

12. Who did Sean Connery play in the 1995 fantasy *First Knight*?

   a. Merlin
   b. King Arthur
   c. Robin Hood
   d. Galahad

13. What 1980s fantasy features beings known as the Gelflings and Skeksis?

a. *Flight of the Navigator*
b. *Ladyhawke*
c. *Labyrinth*
d. *The Dark Crystal*

14. Who played Nanny McPhee in two 2000s fantasy movies?

    a. Emma Thompson
    b. Olivia Colman
    c. Judi Dench
    d. Angela Lansbury

15. Who starred in the 2021 epic medieval fantasy *The Green Knight*?

    a. Jude Law
    b. Dev Patel
    c. Jacob Elordi
    d. Taron Edgerton

16. Which of these actresses did not appear in the 1987 fantasy *The Witches of Eastwick*?

    a. Cher
    b. Michelle Pfeiffer
    c. Susan Sarandon
    d. Meryl Streep

17. Which director, best known for his horror movies, directed the 2018 kids' fantasy movie *The House with the Clock in its Walls*?

    a. Eli Roth
    b. Fede Álvarez
    c. Robert Eggers
    d. Oz Perkins

18. Who played the young girl Edward Scissorhands falls for in Tim Burton's acclaimed fantasy?

    a. Christina Ricci
    b. Kirsten Dunst
    c. Winona Ryder
    d. Alicia Silverstone

ANSWERS

1. B. Christopher Lee. Saruman the White was Sir Christopher Lee's final on-screen role, with *The Battle of the Five Armies* released just six months before his death in 2015 at the age of 93.
2. A. Centaur. Professor Firenze was a centaur who lived in the Forbidden Forest of Hogwarts.
3. D. Tom Cruise. Cruise played Jack in *Legend*, opposite Tim Curry playing the demon-like Darkness.
4. B. *Conan the Barbarian* (1982), D. *The Neverending Story* (1984), C. *Highlander* (1986), A. *Willow* (1988)
5. C. Mel Brooks. Billy Crystal played Miracle Max in the movie, while Peter Cook played a priest with a speech impediment, and Christopher Guest played the count.
6. False. The runtime of the *Lord of the Rings* saga is 558 minutes (nine hrs., 18 mins), while the *Hobbit* movies run 474 minutes (seven hrs., 54 mins).
7. B. Spike Jonze. The movie used a combination of live-action, costume, animatronics, and CGI to bring the creatures to life.
8. A. James McAvoy. All four of the options here appeared in the *Chronicles of Narnia*, but the other three performers were voice actors only.
9. C. Michelle Pfeiffer. The movie was adapted from a novel by Neil Gaiman.
10. B. Zeus. Several British actors took on the mythological roles in the movie, including Olivier as Zeus and Maggie Smith as Thetis.
11. B. Terry Gilliam. Former *Monty Python* star Gilliam is also known for directing *12 Monkeys* and *The Imaginarium of Doctor Parnassus*.
12. B. King Arthur. The film also starred Richard Gere as Lancelot and Julia Ormond as Guinevere.
13. D. *The Dark Crystal*. The Gelflings are the human-like heroes of the movie.
14. A. Emma Thompson. Thompson also wrote the screenplays for the two *Nanny McPhee* movies.
15. B. Dev Patel. *Slumdog Millionaire* star Dev Patel played the knight Gawain in the movie.
16. D. Meryl Streep. Jack Nicholson starred alongside the other three actresses here, plus Veronica Cartwright.

17. A. Eli Roth. Roth is best known for his work on several gore-soaked horrors, including *Cabin Fever* and *Hostel*.
18. C. Winona Ryder. Ryder had previously appeared in another Tim Burton movie, 1988's *Beetlejuice*.

DID YOU KNOW?

Peter Jackson intended to have the opening monologue of his *Lord of the Rings* movies read by Frodo, but when it was decided audiences might presume he survived the trilogy, Galadriel was given the narration instead.

CHAPTER 18
MOVIE MILESTONES

The questions in this chapter are all about firsts, feats, and records — from the very first "talkie" to some extraordinary technological advances.

1. In what year was the first "talkie," Al Jolson's *The Jazz Singer*, released?

   a. 1917
   b. 1922
   c. 1927
   d. 1932

2. What classic story was adapted for cinema in 1925, becoming perhaps the first science fiction film in movie history?

   a. *The Lost World* by Sir Arthur Conan Doyle
   b. *The Time Machine* by H.G. Wells
   c. *20,000 Leagues Under the Sea* by Jules Verne
   d. *The Call of Cthulhu* by H.P. Lovecraft

3. What was the first X-rated movie to win Best Picture at the Oscars?

   a. *The Exorcist*
   b. *Midnight Cowboy*
   c. *A Clockwork Orange*
   d. *Serpico*

4. According to the *Guinness Book of Records*, Richard Attenborough's 1982 epic *Gandhi* set the cinematic record for what?

   a. Longest musical score
   b. Most extras in a movie
   c. Longest credits
   d. Longest screen time for a lead actor

5. What Disney animation was the first film in Oscar history to have three of its musical numbers nominated for the Academy Award for Best Original Song?

   a. *Beauty and the Beast*
   b. *The Little Mermaid*
   c. *Aladdin*
   d. *The Lion King*

6. The 1914 silent movie *Tillie's Punctured Romance* is often said to be the first feature-length film comedy. Who starred in it?

   a. Buster Keaton
   b. Harold Lloyd

    c.   Laurel and Hardy

    d.   Charlie Chaplin

7.   What was the first film in movie history to gross over $1 billion...

    a.   *Titanic*

    b.   *Jurassic World*

    c.   *Harry Potter and the Prisoner of Azkaban*

    d.   *Avengers: Endgame*

8.   ...and what was the first movie in history to gross over $2 billion?

    a.   *Star Wars: Episode 1*

    b.   *Alice in Wonderland*

    c.   *Avatar*

    d.   *Spider-Man: No Way Home*

9.   The 1915 silent epic *The Birth of a Nation* was the first movie to be longer than what length of time?

    a.   An hour

    b.   90 minutes

    c.   Two hours

    d.   Three hours

10. In what decade was the first 3D movie released?

    a.   1920s

    b.   1940s

    c.   1960s

    d.   1980s

11. True or False? Wall-E, in the 2008 Pixar movie of the same name, was the first entirely-computer generated title character in movie history.

12. Released in 1920, *The Cabinet of Dr. Caligari* is said to be the first movie in what genre?

    a.   Action

    b.   Horror

    c.   Biopic

    d.   Documentary

13. The 1984 movie *Red Dawn*, starring Patrick Swayze, was the first movie in history to be given what rating?

    a.   G

    b.   PG-13

c. R

d. NC-17

14. What was the first animated film to be nominated for a Best Picture Oscar...

a. *Snow White*

b. *Bambi*

c. *Beauty and the Beast*

d. *Toy Story 2*

15. ...and in 2010, what became the first animated movie nominated for both Best Animated Feature and Best Picture at the Oscars?

a. *Coraline*

b. *Fantastic Mr. Fox*

c. *The Princess and the Frog*

d. *Up*

16. The 1994 action blockbuster *True Lies* is credited with being the first film with a budget of more than how much?

a. $20 million

b. $50 million

c. $100 million

d. $200 million

17. Each of these movies broke box office records on its release and now ranks among the fastest billion-dollar movies in cinema history. Put them in order of release, starting with the earliest:

a. *Furious 7*

b. *Avatar: The Way of the Water*

c. *Star Wars: The Last Jedi*

d. *Avengers: Endgame*

18. Who made history as being named *Forbes'* highest-earning actor in Hollywood for a record three years in a row in 2013, 2014, and 2015?

a. Mark Wahlberg

b. Dwayne Johnson

c. Johnny Depp

d. Robert Downey, Jr.

ANSWERS

1. C. 1927. Although it was the first talkie, only around 15 minutes of *The Jazz Singer* had live sound, with the remainder made of silent footage and music.
2. A. *The Lost World* by Sir Arthur Conan Doyle. The film used the same stop-motion animation techniques that would later be used in *King Kong* to bring the novel's dinosaurs to life.
3. B. *Midnight Cowboy*. John Schlesinger's 1969 drama is also the *only* X-rated movie to win the Best Picture Oscar, as the certification was discontinued in 1990.
4. B. Most extras in a movie. According to *Guinness*, the 300,000 people who appeared in the epic funeral scene at the end of Gandhi has yet to be beaten.
5. A. *Beauty and the Beast*. Alan Menken and Howard Ashman's songs "Belle," "Be Our Guest," and the film's title track were all up for the award, with "Beauty and the Beast" winning the award.
6. D. Charlie Chaplin. Chaplin's love interest in the movie, Tillie, was played by fellow silent era legend Marie Dressler.
7. A. *Titanic*. It took the James Cameron epic just 72 days to gross $1 billion in 1997.
8. C. *Avatar*. Fewer than ten films have ever grossed more than $2 billion, of which 2009's *Avatar* was the first.
9. D. Three hours. D.W. Griffith's silent epic ran across a full 12 reels of film, with a maximum runtime of 193 minutes.
10. A. 1920s. Incredibly, the world's first 3D movie was *The Power of Love*, released in 1922!
11. False. In fact, that milestone was passed far earlier: cinema's first CGI lead was *Casper* in the 1995 big-screen adaptation of the comics.
12. B. Horror. The movie tells the story of a hypnotist who uses a brainwashed sleepwalker to commit murders.
13. B. PG-13. The PG-13 certificate came into force in July 1984, with the Soviet invasion war movie *Red Dawn* becoming the first film given such a rating.
14. C. *Beauty and the Beast*. The movie was also the first animation to win the Golden Globe for Best Musical or Comedy Motion Picture, and it was the first Disney movie adapted into a Broadway musical.

15. D. *Up*. All four films here were nominated for Best Animated Feature in 2010, with *Up* winning, but *Up* was the only one that was also nominated for overall Best Picture.
16. C. $100 million. Just three years later, *Titanic* would become the first movie to have a budget of $200 million.
17. A. *Furious 7* (2015), C. *Star Wars: The Last Jedi* (2017), D. *Avengers: Endgame* (2019), B. *Avatar: The Way of the Water* (2022).
18. D. Robert Downey, Jr. He earned $75 million in both 2013 and 2014, and a further $80 million in 2015; he became the first actor to top *Forbes'* figures for three consecutive years since Kevin Costner in 1991, 1992, and 1993.

DID YOU KNOW?

Jaws was the first blockbuster to take more than $100 million. Just over 20 years later, 1996's *Independence Day* made that amount in just six days.

CHAPTER 19
COPS & ROBBERS

From comedy crime capers to heist movies, gangster sagas, and prison dramas, cinema has long had an interest in crime and punishment — which is the topic of all questions in this chapter!

1. In what city is the 1987 buddy cop movie *Lethal Weapon* set?

   a. New York
   b. Chicago
   c. Boston
   d. Los Angeles

2. Which legendary Hollywood star played the preacher-turned-serial killer Harry Powell in the 1955 thriller *The Night of the Hunter*?

   a. John Wayne
   b. Robert Mitchum
   c. Gary Cooper
   d. Laurence Olivier

3. Who starred opposite Michael Fassbender as husband-and-wife spies in the 2025 thriller *Black Bag*?

   a. Sandra Bullock
   b. Julia Roberts
   c. Cate Blanchett
   d. Cameron Diaz

4. Who played Mafia don Vito Corleone in 1972's *The Godfather*?

   a. Al Pacino
   b. James Caan
   c. Robert De Niro
   d. Marlon Brando

5. Steve Buscemi's character Carl Showalter meets an infamously grisly end in what 1996 crime comedy drama?

   a. *Pulp Fiction*
   b. *Fargo*
   c. *Con Air*
   d. *Reservoir Dogs*

6. What 1984 crime epic was released in two versions: a critically acclaimed director's cut that ran to almost four hours, and a two-and-a-quarter-hour theatrical cut — edited and released without the director's input — that was a critical and commercial failure?

a. *The Godfather Part III*
b. *Kiss of the Spider Woman*
c. *Once Upon a Time in America*
d. *Prizzi's Honor*

7. In what decade is the acclaimed police corruption saga *LA Confidential* set?

a. 1910s
b. 1930s
c. 1950s
d. 1970s

8. Who won an Oscar for his performance as lawyer Atticus Finch in the 1962 adaptation of *To Kill a Mockingbird*?

a. Paul Newman
b. Gregory Peck
c. James Stewart
d. Montgomery Clift

9. Which of these actors did not star in *Pulp Fiction*?

a. Harvey Keitel
b. Ving Rhames
c. Christopher Walken
d. Michael Madsen

10. The legal thrillers *Runaway Jury, The Pelican Brief,* and *The Client* are all based on novels by which author?

a. John Grisham
b. Tom Clancy
c. James Patterson
d. Michael Crichton

11. Which of these actresses did not appear in the 2018 heist movie *Ocean's 8*?

a. Sandra Bullock
b. Anne Hathaway
c. Cate Blanchett
d. Julia Roberts

12. Who played Bonnie to Warren Beatty's Clyde in the 1967 classic biopic?

a. Lauren Bacall
b. Faye Dunaway
c. Shirley MacLaine
d. Ellen Burstyn

13. In what 1974 crime noir did Jack Nicholson star as private investigator Jake Gittes?

a. *Chinatown*
b. *Mean Streets*
c. *Klute*
d. *The Conversation*

14. Who played the character Ellis "Red" Redding, who narrates *The Shawshank Redemption*?

a. Tim Robbins
b. Clancy Brown
c. Morgan Freeman
d. James Whitmore

15. What is the first name of Al Pacino's title character in the 1973 crime drama *Serpico*?

a. Alan
b. James
c. Frank
d. Craig

16. Who plays the boss of hitmen Colin Farrell and Brendan Gleeson in the 2008 black comedy *In Bruges*?

a. Ralph Fiennes
b. Colin Firth
c. Hugh Grant
d. Michael Gambon

17. True or False? The partly spoken theme to the 1971 crime thriller *Shaft* won the Academy Award for Best Song.

18. Put these prison dramas in order, starting with the earliest:

a. *Cool Hand Luke*
b. *The Green Mile*
c. *Escape from Alcatraz*
d. *In the Name of the Father*

ANSWERS

1. D. Los Angeles. Mel Gibson and Danny Glover play mismatched LAPD officers in the *Lethal Weapon* series.
2. B. Robert Mitchum. Both Cooper and Olivier were considered for the role, but Mitchum ended up winning the part.
3. C. Cate Blanchett. Set in the intricate world of British espionage, the acclaimed spy thriller was directed by Steven Soderbergh.
4. D. Marlon Brando. Robert De Niro reprised the role of Vito in *The Godfather Part II* in 1974.
5. B. Fargo. (Spoiler alert—Showalter's body is disposed of in a woodchipper!)
6. C. *Once Upon a Time in America.* Sergio Leone's film was originally envisaged as a two-part epic, consisting of a pair of three-hour movies, but he was convinced to rework it into a single release, cut to 229 minutes. The US distributors further cut it to just 139 minutes, without Leone's involvement, but this version was a critical and commercial failure.
7. C. 1950s. The movie is set in 1953.
8. B. Gregory Peck. James Stewart was offered the role but turned it down.
9. D. Michael Madsen. A frequent collaborator of Tarantino, Madsen did appear in *Reservoir Dogs* (along with Keitel) but not *Pulp Fiction*.
10. A. John Grisham. Other films based on Grisham's novels include *A Time to Kill* and *The Rainmaker*.
11. D. Julia Roberts. Roberts had appeared in the earlier *Oceans* movies opposite George Clooney and Brad Pitt but not the 2018 all-female installment, *Oceans 8*.
12. B. Faye Dunaway. Shirley MacLaine, Jane Fonda, Cher, and Natalie Wood were also considered for the part.
13. A. Chinatown. The movie was nominated for 11 Academy Awards, with Nicholson scoring a Best Actor nomination.
14. C. Morgan Freeman. All four actors appeared in the movie, but it was Freeman who both played Red in the movie and acted as its narrator.
15. C. Frank. The movie was a biopic of real-life New York police officer and corruption whistleblower Frank Serpico.
16. A. Ralph Fiennes. *In Bruges* was the first feature-length movie by *Three Billboards* filmmaker Martin McDonagh.

17. True. Isaac Hayes, who recorded the track, went on to become the first African-American composer to win an Academy Award.
18. A. *Cool Hand Luke* (1967), C. *Escape from Alcatraz* (1979), *In the Name of the Father* (1993), *The Green Mile* (1999).

DID YOU KNOW?

Paul Newman didn't really eat 50 hard-boiled eggs in *Cool Hand Luke*. According to Newman's co-star George Kennedy, he only ate around eight in total, with the others spat into a bucket as soon as the director yelled "cut"!

CHAPTER 20
MOVIE MUSICALS

From big screen adaptations of Broadway shows to Disney animations, musicals have been a part of cinema for as long as movies have had sound. This next batch of questions celebrates the songs and shows that have captured our ears over the years.

1. Who choreographed, co-directed, and starred alongside Donald O'Connor and Debbie Reynolds in *Singin' in the Rain*?

    a. Frank Sinatra
    b. Fred Astaire
    c. Elvis Presley
    d. Gene Kelly

2. What 21st-century musical features the songs "Another Day of Sun" and "City of Stars"?

    a. *Emilia Pérez*
    b. *Wicked*
    c. *La La Land*
    d. *The Greatest Showman*

3. "In every job that must be done / There is an element of fun" is the opening line to what song from Disney's *Mary Poppins*?

    a. "A Spoonful of Sugar"
    b. "Feed the Birds"
    c. "Super-cali-fragil-istic-expi-ali-docious"
    d. "Chim Chim Cher-ee"

4. What 1960s Oscar-winning musical features the songs "Consider Yourself," "Be Back Soon," and "Reviewing the Situation"?

    a. *Oliver!*
    b. *My Fair Lady*
    c. *Gigi*
    d. *The Sound of Music*

5. Which of these iconic songs did not feature in the soundtrack to Baz Luhrman's musical *Moulin Rouge!*?

    a. "Material Girl"
    b. "Heroes"
    c. "Vogue"
    d. "Your Song"

6. Put these classic movie musicals in order, starting with the earliest:

    a. *South Pacific*

b. *Fiddler on the Roof*

c. *The Great Ziegfeld*

d. *On the Town*

7. Who memorably performed "The Trolley Song" in the 1944 Christmas musical *Meet Me in St. Louis*?

    a. Judy Garland

    b. Doris Day

    c. Marilyn Monroe

    d. Jean Simmons

8. True or False? The hugely popular movie musicals *Oklahoma!*, *Carousel*, *South Pacific*, *The King and I*, and *The Sound of Music* were all based on Broadway shows by the composing duo Rodgers and Hammerstein.

9. Who was the only star of the 1961 movie adaptation of *West Side Story* who also appeared in Steven Spielberg's 2021 version?

    a. Richard Beymer

    b. Rita Moreno

    c. Marni Nixon

    d. Russ Tamblyn

10. What is the first musical number in 1939's *Wizard of Oz*?

    a. "Ding-Dong! The Witch Is Dead"

    b. "Over the Rainbow"

    c. "You're Off to See the Wizard"

    d. "If I Only Had a Brain"

11. What is the name of Lady Gaga's character in the 2018 adaptation of *A Star is Born*?

    a. Ally

    b. Sally

    c. Kelly

    d. Ellie

12. In which of these movie musicals did Barbra Streisand not appear?

    a. *Yentl*

    b. *Hello, Dolly!*

    c. *Cabaret*

    d. *Funny Girl*

13. Which English actor starred opposite Audrey Hepburn as Professor Henry Higgins in the 1964 musical *My Fair Lady*?

a. Ralph Richardson
b. David Niven
c. Roger Moore
d. Rex Harrison

14. Which of the stars of the 2002 movie musical *Chicago* won an Oscar for their performance?

    a. Renée Zellweger
    b. Catherine Zeta-Jones
    c. John C. Reilly
    d. Queen Latifah

15. Which legendary Hollywood star's musical performances include roles in *Showboat, Annie Get Your Gun, Calamity Jane,* and *Seven Brides for Seven Brothers*?

    a. Howard Keel
    b. Fred Astaire
    c. Dick van Dyke
    d. Frank Sinatra

16. What was the English title of the song from the musical *Emilia Pérez* that won the Academy Award for Best Original Song in 2025?

    a. "The Pupil"
    b. "The Evil"
    c. "The Devil"
    d. "The Email"

17. Who sings the ABBA songs "The Name of the Game" and "I Have a Dream" in the 2008 movie adaptation of the jukebox musical *Mamma Mia!*?

    a. Meryl Streep
    b. Christine Baranski
    c. Amanda Seyfried
    d. Julie Walters

18. Which Oscar-winner played slick record executive Curtis Taylor, Jr. in the 2006 movie adaptation of the musical *Dreamgirls*?

    a. Will Smith
    b. Jamie Foxx
    c. Forest Whitaker
    d. Cuba Gooding Jr.

ANSWERS

1. D. Gene Kelly. In an early draft of the movie, Gene Kelly's famous solo dance routine to the title track was intended to be a trio performance.
2. C. *La La Land*. The Oscars for both Original Score and Song were two of the six Academy Awards the movie took home from 14 nominations in 2017.
3. A. *A Spoonful of Sugar*. The songs from *Mary Poppins* were written by long-term Disney collaborators, the Sherman Brothers, Robert and Richard.
4. A. *Oliver!* Based on an earlier 1960 stage musical, the film adaptation of *Oliver!* won six Oscars from 11 nominations in 1969.
5. C. "Vogue." As well as "Material Girl," the film also included an adaptation of Madonna's "Like A Virgin," but not "Vogue."
6. C. *The Great Ziegfeld* (1933), D. *On the Town* (1949), A. *South Pacific* (1958), B. *Fiddler on the Roof* (1971).
7. A. Judy Garland. *Meet Me in St. Louis* was directed by Garland's future husband Vincente Minnelli.
8. True. The film adaptations of Rodgers and Hammerstein's work went on to win a total of 15 Academy Awards.
9. B. Rita Moreno. EGOT winner Moreno played Valentina in Spielberg's adaptation, a role created especially for her to return to the film.
10. B. "Over the Rainbow." Dorothy sings the movie's most famous song while still at home on her family's farm, before she journeys to Oz.
11. A. Ally. Lady Gaga plays singer Ally Campana.
12. C. *Cabaret*. The lead role of Sally Bowles in 1972's *Cabaret* was taken by Liza Minnelli.
13. D. Rex Harrison. Harrison had already played the role on Broadway, but Hepburn's casting was controversial, as the original Broadway star, Julie Andrews, had been hotly tipped to get the movie role, too.
14. B. Catherine Zeta-Jones. All four were nominated for Academy Awards, but it was Zeta-Jones who won the Best Supporting Actress Award for her role as Velma Kelly.
15. A. Howard Keel. Keel made his big-screen musical debut in 1950's *Annie Get Your Gun*.

16. B. "The Evil." The track "El Mal" took the Oscar despite stiff competition from the likes of Diane Warren's "The Journey" and "Never Too Late" by Elton John.
17. C. Amanda Seyfried. Seyfried's character Sophie also appears in performances of "Gimme! Gimme! Gimme! (A Man After Midnight)" and "Waterloo."
18. B. Jamie Foxx. Eddie Murphy also appeared in the movie as singer Jimmy "Thunder" Early.

DID YOU KNOW?

The most successful movie musical in cinema history was the 2019 remake of Disney's *The Lion King*, which earned $1.6 billion at the box office.

CHAPTER 21
LEADING LADIES

In the Golden Age of Hollywood, every leading man had his leading lady — but nowadays, not every movie needs a male lead at all! Some of the movie world's greatest actresses and female stars are the subject of the questions in this chapter.

1. Who directed Susan Sarandon and Geena Davis in *Thelma & Louise*?

    a. Steven Spielberg
    b. Robert Zemeckis
    c. Kathryn Bigelow
    d. Ridley Scott

2. True or False? All 12 of Katharine Hepburn's career Oscar nominations were for Best Lead Actress, as she never received a nomination for Supporting Actress.

3. Put these Cate Blanchett movies in order, starting with the earliest:

    a. *Blue Jasmine*
    b. *I'm Not There*
    c. *The Shipping News*
    d. *Nightmare Alley*

4. Which future Oscar winner made her lead debut opposite Tom Cruise in 1996's *Jerry Maguire*?

    a. Nicole Kidman
    b. Renée Zellweger
    c. Naomi Watts
    d. Julianne Moore

5. Which of these actresses did not star in *Steel Magnolias*?

    a. Daryl Hannah
    b. Dolly Parton
    c. Sally Field
    d. Olivia de Haviland

6. Which of these 21st-century movies did not earn Meryl Streep an Oscar nomination?

    a. *The Post*
    b. *Into the Woods*
    c. *The Devil Wears Prada*
    d. *Don't Look Up*

7. Who links the films *Jurassic Park*, *Wild*, and *Marriage Story*?

a. Scarlett Johansson
b. Reese Witherspoon
c. Laura Dern
d. Bryce Dallas Howard

8. Who was the first leading lady to be known as an "It Girl"?

a. Rita Hayworth
b. Clara Bow
c. Jean Harlow
d. Claudette Colbert

9. Whose film roles include Eleanor of Aquitaine, Clara Schumann, the mythological queen Hecuba, and Mary, Queen of Scots?

a. Katharine Hepburn
b. Elizabeth Taylor
c. Grace Kelly
d. Julie Christie

10. Which of these actresses holds the record for the longest Oscar-winning performance, with a time of two hours and 23 minutes on-screen?

a. Cate Blanchett
b. Judy Garland
c. Meryl Streep
d. Vivien Leigh

11. In which of her movies did Sandra Bullock play a character named Dr. Ryan Stone?

a. *Speed*
b. *Bird Box*
c. *While You Were Sleeping*
d. *Gravity*

12. Who starred as the grief-stricken mother of the family in *Hereditary*?

a. Natalie Portman
b. Angelina Jolie
c. Toni Collette
d. Hilary Swank

13. Which legendary English actress appeared in the drama *The Prime of Miss Jean Brodie*, the comedy *California Suite*, the murder mystery *Death on the Nile*, and the children's movie *Hook*?

a. Maggie Smith
b. Judi Dench
c. Lynn Redgrave
d. Peggy Ashcroft

14. Which of these Hollywood stars was not born in Australia?

a. Rose Byrne
b. Margot Robbie
c. Charlize Theron
d. Mia Wasikowska

15. In 1977, who became the first woman to receive a Lifetime Achievement Award from the American Film Institute?

a. Lilian Gish
b. Elizabeth Taylor
c. Bette Davis
d. Barbara Stanwyck

16. Who starred alongside Dolly Parton and Lily Tomlin in the 1980 comedy *9 to 5*?

a. Debra Winger
b. Jane Fonda
c. Jessica Lange
d. Kathleen Turner

17. True or False? When Glenn Close lost the 2018 Best Actress Oscar to Olivia Colman in *The Favorite*, she became the most Oscar-nominated actress in Hollywood history without a win.

18. Which of these actresses appeared in the original 1984 *Ghostbusters* movie?

a. Michelle Pfeiffer
b. Sigourney Weaver
c. Jodie Foster
d. Dianne Wiest

ANSWERS

1. D. Ridley Scott. *Thelma & Louise* earned him his first Oscar nomination.
2. True. Hepburn's nominations spanned the entirety of her screen career, from her first, for *Morning Glory* in 1934, to her last, for *On Golden Pond*, in 1982.
3. C. *The Shipping News* (2001), B. *I'm Not There* (2007), A. *Blue Jasmine* (2013), D. *Nightmare Alley* (2021).
4. B. Renée Zellweger. Zellweger's role in *Jerry Maguire* was followed by a number of lead performances that have since won her two Oscars.
5. D. Olivia de Haviland. The movie also starred Julia Roberts, Shirley MacLaine, and Olympia Dukakis.
6. D. *Don't Look Up*. Streep played the US president in the 2021 comedy, which earned an Academy Award nomination for Best Picture but no acting nominations.
7. C. Laura Dern. Dern starred alongside Reese Witherspoon in *Wild* and Scarlett Johansson in *Marriage Story*, but only she connects all three titles here.
8. B. Clara Bow. Clara Bow was an early star of silent movies whose role as a shop girl in the 1927 silent *It* earned her the nickname the "It Girl."
9. A. Katharine Hepburn. Those were Hepburn's roles in the movies *The Lion in Winter* (1968), *Song of Love* (1947), *The Trojan Women* (1971), and *Mary of Scotland* (1936).
10. D. Vivien Leigh. This was the length of Leigh's screentime in *Gone with the Wind*, the movie for which she won the 1939 Best Actress Oscar.
11. D. *Gravity*. Bullock's role as an astronaut trapped in space earned her an Oscar nomination.
12. C. Toni Collette. Ari Aster's 2018 horror became the groundbreaking independent studio A24's highest-grossing movie at the time.
13. A. Maggie Smith. Smith won Oscars for her performances in *The Prime of Miss Jean Brodie* and *California Suite*.
14. C. Charlize Theron. Theron was born in South Africa in 1975.
15. C. Bette Davis. All four of these legendary actresses have been awarded the AFI's Lifetime Achievement Award, but Davis was first.
16. B. Jane Fonda. The movie was a box office smash hit and further established its three stars as legendary entertainers.

17. True. Close's role in 2018's *The Wife* was her seventh unsuccessful Oscar nomination; she has since been nominated an eighth time, for 2020's *Hillbilly Elegy*.
18. B. Sigourney Weaver. Best known as a dramatic actress at the time, Weaver reportedly won the role by comically pretending to transform into a dog during her audition!

DID YOU KNOW?

English actress Hermione Baddeley was nominated for a Best Supporting Actress Oscar for just two minutes and 19 seconds of screen time in the 1959 British drama *Room at the Top*. Hers is the shortest Oscar-nominated performance in history!

CHAPTER 22
ANIMATION

In the century or so since Walt Disney's *Snow White*, the first feature-length animation, 11 of the 50 highest-grossing movies of all time are animated features!

1. True or False? Walt Disney's *Snow White* was so successful that it was not only the biggest film of the year but, for a time, it held the record as the most successful sound film of all time.

2. Which animated movie studio produces the *Shrek* films?
    a. DreamWorks
    b. Disney
    c. Pixar
    d. Aardman

3. Maleficent is the main antagonist in which Disney animated movie?
    a. *Cinderella*
    b. *Snow White*
    c. *Sleeping Beauty*
    d. *Tangled*

4. *Dreams Come True* and *A Twist in Time* were 21st-century sequels to what classic Disney movie?
    a. *The Sword in the Stone*
    b. *Cinderella*
    c. *Snow White*
    d. *Beauty and the Beast*

5. What kind of animal was the main character in the 2024 animated movie *Flow*?
    a. Cat
    b. Turtle
    c. Duck
    d. Shark

6. Put these classic Disney villains in order, starting with the earliest to make her appearance on the big screen:
    a. Ursula the Sea Witch
    b. Lady Tremaine
    c. Mother Gothel
    d. The Evil Queen

7. Which English actor starred opposite Roger Rabbit in the 1989 partly animated movie?

a. Michael Gambon
b. Michael Caine
c. Ben Kingsley
d. Bob Hoskins

8. Put these Hayao Miyazaki movies in order, starting with the earliest released:

a. *Howl's Moving Castle*
b. *Princess Mononoke*
c. *Spirited Away*
d. *The Boy and the Heron*

9. In what 2016 animated movie did Reese Witherspoon voice a pig named Rosita?

a. *Sing*
b. *Flushed Away*
c. *Zootopia*
d. *How to Train Your Dragon*

10. In a memorable scene in Disney's *Dumbo,* the eponymous baby elephant gets drunk after drinking what?

a. Red wine
b. Whisky
c. Gin
d. Champagne

11. In *Finding Nemo,* what kind of creature is Bruce?

a. Starfish
b. Clownfish
c. Sea turtle
d. Shark

12. Who is Pongo in a well-known Disney animated movie?

a. A Dalmatian in *One Hundred and One Dalmatians*
b. A mouse in *The Rescuers*
c. A fox in *The Fox and the Hound*
d. A lion in *The Lion King*

13. True or False? British actress Kathryn Beaumont, who voiced Alice in Walt Disney's 1951 animated adaptation of *Alice in Wonderland,* also voiced Wendy in Disney's *Peter Pan.*

14. Who voices Puss in Boots in the *Shrek* movies and spinoff franchise?

    a. Javier Bardem
    b. Gael García Bernal
    c. Antonio Banderas
    d. Benicio del Toro

15. Which of these actors did not voice a character in *Monsters, Inc.*?

    a. Steve Buscemi
    b. Harvey Keitel
    c. John Goodman
    d. James Coburn

16. The legendary American entertainer Cliff Edwards — known as Ukulele Ike — provided the voice for what Disney character?

    a. Jiminy Cricket in *Pinocchio*
    b. The Sorcerer in *Fantasia*
    c. Captain Hook in *Peter Pan*
    d. Baloo in *The Jungle Book*

17. What kind of creature is Archimedes in Disney's *The Sword in the Stone*?

    a. A frog
    b. A wolf
    c. An owl
    d. A dog

18. True or False? The *Despicable Me* franchise is now the most successful animated franchise in movie history.

ANSWERS

1. True. The movie grossed $8 million on its release (equivalent to almost $200 million today) against a budget of just $1.5 million, and it was the most successful movie of both 1937 *and* 1938.
2. A. DreamWorks. Steven Spielberg originally intended to produce an animated version of William Steig's 1990 children's picture book *Shrek!* before the project was taken over by CGI animators at DreamWorks in 1995.
3. C. *Sleeping Beauty*. The character later featured in a series of live-action movies, played by Angelina Jolie.
4. B. *Cinderella*. The movies were released straight-to-video in 2002 and 2007.
5. A. Cat. The movie tells the story of a cat who takes refuge on a boat alongside several other animals after their home is destroyed by a flood.
6. D. The Evil Queen (*Snow White*, 1937), B. Lady Tremaine (*Cinderella*, 1950), A. Ursula the Sea Witch (*The Little Mermaid*, 1989), C. Mother Gothel (*Tangled*, 2010).
7. D. Bob Hoskins. A host of other 1980s A-listers were considered for the role of Eddie in *Who Framed Roger Rabbit?*, including Harrison Ford, Jack Nicholson, Sylvester Stallone, Robert Redford, and Bill Murray.
8. B. *Princess Mononoke* (1997), C. *Spirited Away* (2001), A. *Howl's Moving Castle* (2004), D. *The Boy and the Heron* (2023).
9. A. *Sing*. Witherspoon's character is the mother of 25 piglets, several of the voices for which were provided by the children of the movie's director, Garth Jennings.
10. D. Champagne. Dumbo ends up hallucinating pink elephants in his drunken stupor!
11. D. Shark. Voiced by Dame Edna actor Barry Humphries, Bruce is a great white shark.
12. A. A Dalmatian in *One Hundred and One Dalmatians*. Pongo is the partner of Perdita.
13. True. Beaumont also provided live-action model work as a reference for the *Peter Pan* animators.
14. C. Antonio Banderas. Spanish actor Antonio Banderas has appeared as Puss in Boots in all but the first *Shrek* movie, as well as two *Puss in Boots* spinoff movies.

15. B. Harvey Keitel. Steve Buscemi voiced the chameleon-like Randall, John Goodman played Sully, and Hollywood legend James Coburn voiced Monsters, Inc. CEO Henry Waternoose.
16. A. Jiminy Cricket in *Pinocchio*. Captain Hook was voiced by Hans Conried, while Disney legend Phil Harris provided the voice of Baloo (as well as Thomas O'Malley in *The Aristocats* and Little John in Disney's *Robin Hood*).
17. C. An owl. Archimedes is the wizard Merlin's highly educated pet owl.
18. True. The *Despicable Me* and *Minions* movies have now earned over $5.3 billion at the box office—more than the *Shrek* ($4 billion), *Toy Story* ($3.2 billion), and *Ice Age* ($3.2 billion) franchises.

DID YOU KNOW?

Not including re-releases, the most successful animated movie of all time is *Inside Out 2*, which earned $1.6 billion at the box office!

CHAPTER 23
COMEDY CLASSICS

The likes of the Marx Brothers, the Keystone Cops, and Charlie Chaplin were making early cinemagoers laugh more than a century ago, and movies have kept us laughing ever since. This next set of questions is all about classic comedies.

1. In what year did Charlie Chaplin debut his iconic Little Tramp character?

    a. 1904
    b. 1914
    c. 1924
    d. 1935

2. What 2000s comedy featured characters named Brick Tamland, Brian Fantana, and Veronica Corningstone?

    a. *The Hangover*
    b. *Step Brothers*
    c. *Anchorman*
    d. *Talladega Nights*

3. In what city is the 1959 comedy *Some Like It Hot* set?

    a. Paris
    b. Chicago
    c. Los Angeles
    d. Havana

4. Who starred opposite Dustin Hoffman in *Tootsie*?

    a. Jessica Lange
    b. Susan Sarandon
    c. Meryl Streep
    d. Geena Davis

5. Which legendary comic actor took on multiple roles in the 1964 comedy *Dr. Strangelove or: How I Learned to Stop Worrying and Love the Bomb*?

    a. Groucho Marx
    b. Bob Hope
    c. Dudley Moore
    d. Peter Sellers

6. Put these Robin Williams comedies in order, starting with the earliest:

    a. *The Birdcage*
    b. *Good Morning, Vietnam*

c. *Aladdin*
d. *The World According to Garp*

7. Which of these Hollywood actors was a *Saturday Night Live* castmate in the 1985–86 season?

   a. Robert Downey Jr.
   b. Paul Rudd
   c. Owen Wilson
   d. Martin Lawrence

8. Which acclaimed English actor starred alongside Tim Allen in the 1999 sci-fi spoof *Galaxy Quest*?

   a. Alan Rickman
   b. Michael Gambon
   c. Kenneth Branagh
   d. Derek Jacobi

9. Which of these legendary actors did not have a cameo role in the 1979 *Muppet Movie*?

   a. Bob Hope
   b. Frank Sinatra
   c. Telly Savalas
   d. Orson Welles

10. Who starred as Private Benjamin in the 1980 comedy of the same name?

    a. Diane Keaton
    b. Goldie Hawn
    c. Bette Midler
    d. Carrie Fisher

11. The controversial Monty Python comedy *Life of Brian* was a parody of the life of which historical figure?

    a. Henry VIII
    b. Jesus
    c. Napoleon
    d. Adolf Hitler

12. Which sports star appeared as a member of the flight crew in the classic comedy *Airplane!*?

    a. Kareem Abdul-Jabbar

b. Muhammad Ali

c. André the Giant

d. Chuck Norris

13. *The Legend of Curly's Gold* was the 1994 sequel to what classic comedy?

a. *The Three Amigos*

b. *The Naked Gun*

c. *City Slickers*

d. *The Addams Family*

14. Who won an Oscar for his supporting role in the 1988 comedy *A Fish Called Wanda*?

a. Tim Robbins

b. Kevin Kline

c. Pill Bullman

d. Billy Crystal

15. Who played the waspish mother superior whose convent Whoopi Goldberg joins in the 1992 comedy *Sister Act*?

a. Vanessa Redgrave

b. Miranda Richardson

c. Maggie Smith

d. Helen Mirren

16. Put these classic comedies of the 1970s, '80s, and '90s in order, starting with the earliest:

a. *My Cousin Vinny*

b. *Annie Hall*

c. *M*A*S*H*

d. *Planes, Trains and Automobiles*

17. Which Hollywood legend starred in the 1940s comedies *His Girl Friday*, *The Philadelphia Story*, *Arsenic and Old Lace*, and *Charade*?

a. James Stewart

b. Clark Gable

c. Cary Grant

d. David Niven

18. Which of these actors did not star in the 2006 dark comedy *Little Miss Sunshine*?

a. Toni Collette
b. Steve Carell
c. Alan Arkin
d. Bill Murray

ANSWERS

1. B. 1914. Chaplin's Tramp debuted in a 1914 Keystone comedy called *Kid Auto Races at Venice*.
2. C. *Anchorman*. Those were the roles played by comic actors Steve Carell, Paul Rudd, and Christina Applegate, respectively, opposite Will Ferrell as Ron Burgundy.
3. B. Chicago. The plot of the movie revolves around two musicians who inadvertently witness a St Valentine's Day Massacre-style gangster assassination in Chicago.
4. A. Jessica Lange. Lange won the Best Supporting Actress Oscar for her performance.
5. D. Peter Sellers. Sellers played Lionel Mandrake, President Merkin Muffley, and Dr. Strangelove himself in the film.
6. D. *The World According to Garp* (1982), B. *Good Morning, Vietnam* (1987), C. *Aladdin* (1992), A. *The Birdcage* (1996).
7. A. Robert Downey Jr. Alongside the likes of Randy Quaid and Anthony Michael Hall, Downey Jr. was one of a number of younger and more established stars recruited by *Saturday Night Live* in the mid-1980s.
8. A. Alan Rickman. Rickman played a stage actor struggling to find more serious work after years spent playing an alien on a television serial.
9. B. Frank Sinatra. Bob Hope played an ice cream vendor, Telly Savalas was a tough guy at the El Sleezo Café, and Orson Welles played a Hollywood executive.
10. B. Goldie Hawn. Hawn was nominated for an Oscar for her role in Howard Zieff's classic comedy.
11. B. Jesus. The film told the story of a young Judean man, played by Monty Python castmate Graham Chapman, who was born on the same day as, and is consequently mistaken for, the Messiah.
12. A. Kareen Abdul-Jabbar. The former NBA star played First Officer Roger Murdock.
13. *City Slickers*. The sequel again starred Billy Crystal and Jack Palance, who had won an Oscar for his performance in the original 1991 film.
14. B. Kevin Kline. The movie also starred John Cleese (whose screenplay also earned an Oscar nomination), Jamie Lee Curtis, and Michael Palin.

15. C. Maggie Smith. Goldberg and Smith starred together in both *Sister Act* and its sequel, *Back in the Habit*.
16. C. *M*A*S*H* (1970), B. *Annie Hall* (1977) D. *Planes, Trains and Automobiles* (1987), A. *My Cousin Vinny* (1992).
17. C. Cary Grant. Although he began his career as a dramatic actor, Grant was known for his excellent comic timing and delivery, and he starred in a string of screwball comedies.
18. D. Bill Murray. The role of Frank in the movie had been written for Bill Murray but eventually went to Steve Carell.

DID YOU KNOW?

The highest-grossing comedy of all time is Greta Gerwig's 2023 *Barbie* movie, which took $1.4 billion at the box office.

CHAPTER 24
THRILLS, SPILLS & CHILLS

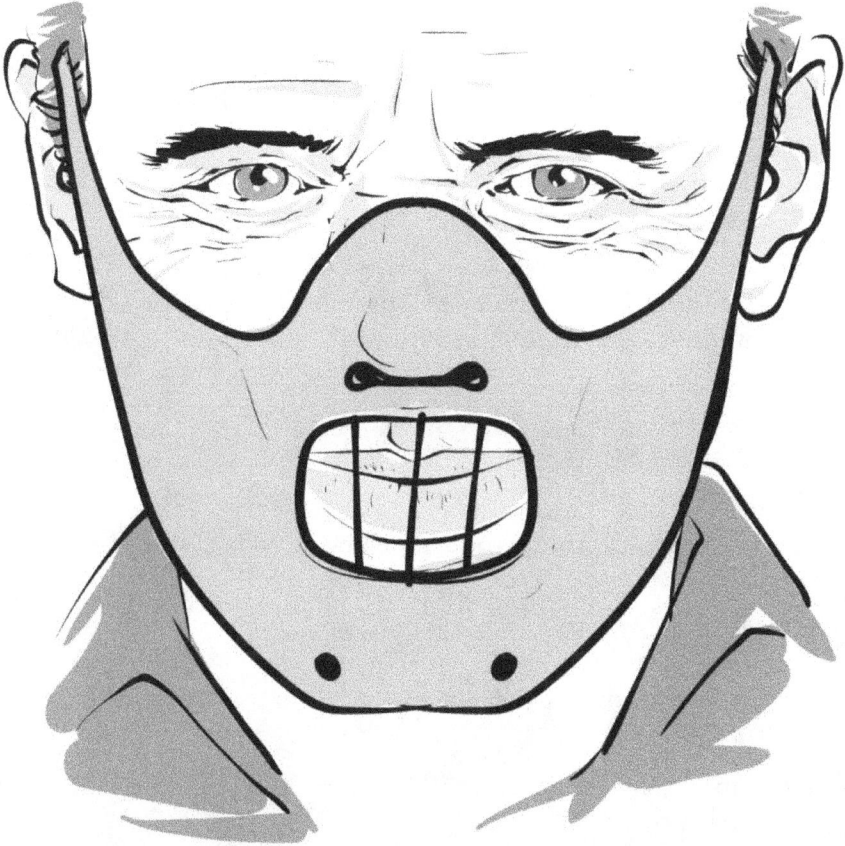

As well as make us laugh and cry, movies can raise our heart rate and have us fearing for what comes next! The questions in this chapter are dedicated to some of cinema's greatest thrillers.

1. Anthony Hopkins won an Oscar for his performance as Hannibal Lecter in *The Silence of the Lambs* — despite only being on screen in the movie for a little under what length of time?

    a. 25 minutes
    b. 35 minutes
    c. 45 minutes
    d. 55 minutes

2. Who starred opposite Sharon Stone in the 1992 thriller *Basic Instinct*?

    a. Sean Penn
    b. Stephen Baldwin
    c. Michael Douglas
    d. Willem Dafoe

3. The 1957 novel *The Executioners* by John D. MacDonald has twice been adapted for cinema, in 1962 and 1991, under what title?

    a. *Fatal Attraction*
    b. *Cape Fear*
    c. *12 Angry Men*
    d. *Pacific Heights*

4. Put these classic Hollywood thrillers in order, starting with the earliest:

    a. *Dog Day Afternoon*
    b. *North by Northwest*
    c. *The Manchurian Candidate*
    d. *Gaslight*

5. What animal is responsible for the titular *Outbreak* in the 1995 Dustin Hoffman movie?

    a. Monkey
    b. Bat
    c. Parrot
    d. Cat

6. What kind of natural disaster is featured in the 1997 action movie *Dante's Peak*?

a. Avalanche
b. Flood
c. Volcano
d. Tsunami

7. What classic Bond movie is set almost entirely on a European train?

   a. *Goldfinger*
   b. *From Russia with Love*
   c. *You Only Live Twice*
   d. *On Her Majesty's Secret Service*

8. Who starred in Martin Scorsese's acclaimed 2010 thriller *Shutter Island*?

   a. Christian Bale
   b. Jake Gyllenhaal
   c. Ryan Gosling
   d. Leonardo Di Caprio

9. True or False? Natalie Portman studied ballet for a year in preparation for her Oscar-winning role in the Darren Aronofsky thriller *Black Swan*.

10. What classic disaster movie was the highest-grossing film of 1974?

    a. *The Poseidon Adventure*
    b. *The Towering Inferno*
    c. *Earthquake*
    d. *Airport*

11. Who starred in the 2011 dark psychological drama *We Need to Talk About Kevin*?

    a. Emma Thompson
    b. Tilda Swinton
    c. Julianne Moore
    d. Toni Collette

12. True or False? The 1998 disaster movie *Armageddon* was narrated by Orson Welles.

13. Which future Oscar winner directed the 1990s and early-2000s thrillers *Following*, *Memento*, and *Insomnia*?

    a. Christopher Nolan
    b. Steven Spielberg

c. Paul Thomas Anderson
d. Joel and Ethan Coen

14. What affliction does Audrey Hepburn's character have in the 1967 thriller *Wait Until Dark*?

a. She's paralyzed
b. She's blind
c. She's deaf
d. She's mute

15. The classic 1949 noir thriller *The Third Man* is set in what European city?

a. London
b. Berlin
c. Madrid
d. Vienna

16. Which of these actresses has not portrayed the character Lisbeth Salander on the big screen, in one of the *Girl with the Dragon Tattoo* series of films?

a. Rooney Mara
b. Julia Stiles
c. Claire Foy
d. Noomi Rapace

17. Who starred opposite Ben Affleck in the 2014 thriller *Gone Girl*?

a. Emily Blunt
b. Rosamund Pike
c. Florence Pugh
d. Jessica Chastain

18. In the 1941 movie of the same name, what is The Maltese Falcon?

a. Aircraft
b. Statuette
c. Manuscript
d. Bird

ANSWERS

1. A. 25 minutes. In fact, Hopkins' screen time comes in at just 24 minutes and 52 seconds, making it the second-shortest Best Actor Oscar–winning performance in the history of the award.
2. C. Michael Douglas. Michael Douglas played the detective who falls for the prime suspect in a murder case, played by Stone.
3. B. *Cape Fear*. The 1962 adaptation starred Gregory Peck and Robert Mitchum, while the 1991 version starred Nick Nolte and Robert De Niro.
4. D. *Gaslight* (1944), B. *North by Northwest* (1959), C. *The Manchurian Candidate* (1962), A. *Dog Day Afternoon* (1975).
5. A. Monkey. The monkey in *Outbreak* was played by a white-headed capuchin named Betsy, who also appeared as Ross' pet monkey Marcel in the sitcom *Friends*.
6. C. Volcano. The movie starred Pierce Brosnan as a volcanologist and Linda Hamilton as the local mayor.
7. B. *From Russia with Love*. 1963's *From Russia with Love* was the second Bond movie.
8. D. Leonardo Di Caprio. The movie also starred Mark Ruffalo, Ben Kingsley, and Michelle Williams.
9. True. Portman had studied ballet as a child but took to an intensive year-long dance training regimen in preparation for the movie.
10. B. *The Towering Inferno*. Featuring an all-star cast, *The Towering Inferno* grossed more than $200 million at the box office.
11. B. Tilda Swinton. Adapted from the novel by Lionel Shriver, Swinton was nominated for an Oscar for her performance.
12. False. In fact, it was narrated by Charlton Heston.
13. A. Christopher Nolan. These were Nolan's first three feature films, released in 1998, 2000, and 2002, respectively.
14. B. She's blind. Hepburn plays a blind woman trapped in her basement apartment by dangerous drug-smuggling gangsters.
15. D. Vienna. The film is set in postwar Austria.
16. B. Julia Stiles. Noomi Rapace played Lisbeth in the original Swedish adaptations of Steig Larsson's novels *The Girl with the Dragon Tattoo*, *The Girl Who Played with Fire*, and *The Girl Who Kicked the Hornets' Nest* in 2009. Rooney Mara took over the role for the 2011 English-language version of *The Girl with the Dragon Tattoo*, and Claire Foy

starred in 2018's *The Girl in the Spider's Web*, written after Larsson's death in 2004.

17. B. Rosamund Pike. Pike played Affleck's wife Amy.
18. B. Statuette. The eponymous falcon is a highly valuable jewel-encrusted ornament.

DID YOU KNOW?

He might be "The Master of Suspense," but Alfred Hitchcock's entry into the movie world was far more sedate: he began his film career as a desk clerk and title-card writer!

CHAPTER 25
FILM DEBUTS

Not all A-list actors and actresses hit the ground running, and many end up making their big-screen debuts in limited roles, background performances, and even uncredited appearances. Some of cinema's most noteworthy debuts, large and small, are the subject of this next set of questions.

1. What is the name of the character played by Jamie Lee Curtis in her big-screen debut, *Halloween*?

   a. Laurie
   b. Corie
   c. Dorie
   d. Averie

2. Jake Gyllenhaal began his acting career while still a child, making his debut appearance on screen at age 11 in what 1990s comedy?

   a. *Sister Act*
   b. *Mrs. Doubtfire*
   c. *City Slickers*
   d. *Liar Liar*

3. In what horror franchise did Johnny Depp make his feature film debut?

   a. *I Know What You Did Last Summer*
   b. *Friday the 13th*
   c. *Scream*
   d. *A Nightmare on Elm Street*

4. Who made her debut film appearance in a 1983 festive Australian drama called *Bush Christmas*?

   a. Nicole Kidman
   b. Naomi Watts
   c. Charlize Theron
   d. Margot Robbie

5. Directed by future *Lord of the Rings* director Peter Jackson, which was Kate Winslet's first movie?

   a. *Sense and Sensibility*
   b. *Hamlet*
   c. *Heavenly Creatures*
   d. *Titanic*

6. True or False? Tom Hanks' film debut was in a 1980 slasher movie.

7. Kevin Kline made his feature film debut in what classic Meryl Streep drama?

    a. *The Deer Hunter*
    b. *Kramer vs. Kramer*
    c. *The French Lieutenant's Woman*
    d. *Sophie's Choice*

8. Which *Friends* star's debut movie credit was in the 1993 horror *Leprechaun*?

    a. Courtney Cox
    b. Jennifer Aniston
    c. Lisa Kudrow
    d. Matthew Perry

9. Which future Oscar-winning actor made his debut appearance on film in an uncredited role as a "Man on the beach with a drink" in a 1987 comedy called *Hunk*?

    a. George Clooney
    b. Brad Pitt
    c. Matt Dillon
    d. Ben Affleck

10. Whom did Arnold Schwarzenegger play in his movie acting debut?

    a. Achilles
    b. Hercules
    c. Odysseus
    d. Perseus

11. Which of these legendary actresses was nominated for an Oscar for her debut film in 1944?

    a. Vivien Leigh
    b. Joan Crawford
    c. Lauren Bacall
    d. Angela Lansbury

12. True or False? Spencer Tracy and Humphrey Bogart made their feature film debuts in the same film.

13. What was unusual about Robert De Niro's big-screen debut in the 1965 drama *Three Rooms in Manhattan*?

    a. The movie wasn't in English
    b. His role was cut

c. It was Al Pacino's film debut, too

d. It was directed by his brother

14. How old was Steven Spielberg when he wrote, produced, directed, edited, and composed the music for his 1964 first feature-length movie, *Firelight*?

   a. 17
   b. 22
   c. 27
   d. 31

15. Sigourney Weaver's film debut was a minor role in what 1977 Woody Allen comedy?

   a. *Annie Hall*
   b. *Manhattan*
   c. *The Purple Rose of Cairo*
   d. *Hannah and Her Sisters*

16. Put these Hollywood A-listers in order by the date of their film debut, beginning with the earliest:

   a. Meryl Streep
   b. Julia Roberts
   c. Susan Sarandon
   d. Cameron Diaz

17. What classic Bogart and Bacall romance was Lauren Bacall's first movie role?

   a. *Two Guys from Milwaukee*
   b. *To Have and Have Not*
   c. *Key Largo*
   d. *The Big Sleep*

18. True or False? *The Wizard of Oz* was Judy Garland's first film role.

ANSWERS

1. A. Laurie. Jamie Lee Curtis had made a handful of television appearances before landing the role of Laurie Strode in John Carpenter's slasher movie in 1978.
2. C. *City Slickers*. Gyllenhaal played the young son of Mitch Robbins in the film, played by Billy Crystal.
3. D. *A Nightmare on Elm Street*. Depp made his debut in the original movie in 1984.
4. A. Nicole Kidman. Kidman starred in a string of Australian movies before her move to Hollywood in the late 1980s.
5. C. *Heavenly Creatures*. Winslet followed her debut in *Heavenly Creatures* with her roles in *Sense and Sensibility*, *Hamlet*, and *Titanic*.
6. True. Hanks played the character Elliot in the 1980 horror *He Knows You're Alone*.
7. D. *Sophie's Choice*. Kline played Sophie's American lover, Nathan, in the film.
8. B. Jennifer Aniston. Aniston played the character Tory, opposite a demonic Warwick Davis, in the first *Leprechaun* movie.
9. B. Brad Pitt. In fact, Pitt went uncredited in his first four films.
10. B. Hercules. Schwarzenegger's acting debut was in a film called *Hercules in New York*.
11. D. Angela Lansbury. Lansbury was nominated for Best Supporting Actress for her debut in *Gaslight* and went on to be nominated again for only her third film role, *The Picture of Dorian Grey*.
12. True. Tracy and Bogart made their feature debuts opposite one another in John Ford's 1930 comedy *Up the River*.
13. A. The movie wasn't in English. *Three Rooms in Manhattan* was a French-language adaptation of Georges Simenon's novel *Trois Chambres à Manhattan*.
14. A. 17. Having made several short films, *Firelight* was Spielberg's feature-length debut.
15. A. *Annie Hall*. Weaver played Allen's character Alvy's date at the very end of the film.
16. C. Susan Sarandon (*Joe*, 1970), A. Meryl Streep (*Julia*, 1977), B. Julia Roberts (*Firehouse*, 1987), D. Cameron Diaz (*The Mask*, 1994).
17. B. *To Have and Have Not*. The pair began their long relationship during the filming of 1944's *To Have and Have Not* and married the following year.

18. False. In fact, despite being just 16 in *The Wizard of Oz*, the film was already Garland's seventh feature film performance.

DID YOU KNOW?

To date, a little over a dozen actors have won Oscars for their feature film debut, including Lupita Nyong'o—who won Best Supporting Actress for *12 Years A Slave* before she had even finished drama school!

CHAPTER 26
LITERARY ADAPTATIONS

Movie actors and directors have long taken an interest in adapting existing stories and books to the big screen, from classic horrors in the silent era to global best-sellers in the 21st century. Some of cinema's most popular literary adaptations are the subject of this next set of questions.

1. Which of these actresses did not star alongside Saoirse Ronan in Greta Gerwig's 2019 adaptation of *Little Women*?

   a. Emma Watson
   b. Laura Dern
   c. Amanda Seyfried
   d. Meryl Streep

2. Audrey Hepburn starred opposite Henry Fonda in an acclaimed 1956 adaptation of which classic Russian novel?

   a. *War and Peace*
   b. *The Master and Margarita*
   c. *Crime and Punishment*
   d. *Anna Karenina*

3. What classic science fiction novel was adapted for radio in 1938 and then twice for cinema in 1953 and 2005?

   a. *The Day of the Triffids*
   b. *The Island of Doctor Moreau*
   c. *The Invisible Man*
   d. *The War of the Worlds*

4. Emma Thompson became the first Oscar-winning actor to also win an Oscar for Best Adapted Screenplay for her work in what Jane Austen adaptation?

   a. *Pride and Prejudice*
   b. *Emma*
   c. *Mansfield Park*
   d. *Sense and Sensibility*

5. Who adapted his own novel *The Godfather* for the big screen in 1972?

   a. John Grisham
   b. John Updike
   c. Mario Puzo
   d. William Faulkner

6. Put these books brought to the big screen in order by the year in which their movie versions were released, starting with the earliest:

    a. *A Clockwork Orange*
    b. *Mary Poppins*
    c. *Breakfast at Tiffany's*
    d. *Rosemary's Baby*

7. True or False? When the novel *Catch-22* was adapted for cinema in 1970, its author Joseph Heller adapted the screenplay himself.

8. Which of these movies was adapted from a book by Chuck Palahniuk?

    a. *Fight Club*
    b. *American Psycho*
    c. *Requiem for a Dream*
    d. *Trainspotting*

9. Which of these literary Disney animations was based on a book written back in 1865?

    a. *Peter Pan*
    b. *Alice in Wonderland*
    c. *One Hundred and One Dalmatians*
    d. *The Jungle Book*

10. Which of these '90s movies was not based on a novel by Michael Crichton?

    a. *Sphere*
    b. *Disclosure*
    c. *Congo*
    d. *Patriot Games*

11. Which literary character links the actors Johnny Depp, Gene Wilder, and Timothée Chalamet?

    a. The Mad Hatter
    b. Willy Wonka
    c. Ichabod Crane
    d. Sweeney Todd

12. Who played detective Hercule Poirot in the 1974 all-star adaptation of Agatha Christie's mystery *Murder on the Orient Express*?

    a. Kenneth Branagh
    b. Peter Ustinov

c. Albert Finney
d. Richard Widmark

13. According to the *Guinness Book of Records*, which literary character has been portrayed on screen the most times, in a total of more than 270 adaptations?

    a. Sherlock Holmes
    b. Count Dracula
    c. Miss Marple
    d. Oliver Twist

14. In what Stephen King adaptation does James Caan play the character Paul Sheldon?

    a. *Creepshow*
    b. *Christine*
    c. *Misery*
    d. *The Shining*

15. Which of these Oscar-winning movies was based on a novel by Thomas Keneally?

    a. *The Hours*
    b. *Schindler's List*
    c. *The Remains of the Day*
    d. *The English Patient*

16. True or False? The highest-grossing literary adaptation of the 21st century was *The Return of the King*, from the *Lord of the Rings* trilogy.

17. Which of these actors did not appear in the 2012 *Hunger Games* movie?

    a. Woody Harrelson
    b. Kiefer Sutherland
    c. Stanley Tucci
    d. Toby Jones

18. Who is said to be the most-adapted writer in cinema history, with at least 1,100 big-screen adaptations of their work?

    a. William Shakespeare
    b. Agatha Christie
    c. Charles Dickens
    d. Stephen King

ANSWERS

1. C. Amada Seyfried. The movie had an ensemble cast that also included Timothée Chalamet, Bob Odenkirk, Chris Cooper, and Eliza Scanlen.
2. A. *War and Peace*. Hepburn played Natasha Rostova in the film, alongside Henry Fonda as Count Bezukhov and Mel Ferrer as Prince Andrei.
3. D. *The War of the Worlds*. The 1938 radio adaptation was Orson Welles' infamous version, which caused widespread panic on its broadcast.
4. D. *Sense and Sensibility*. Thompson also played Elinor Dashwood in the film and was nominated for an Oscar for her performance, too.
5. C. Mario Puzo. Puzo won an Oscar for his screenplay. He also wrote the screenplay for 1978's *Superman* and the 1980 sequel.
6. C. *Breakfast at Tiffany's* (Truman Capote, 1961), B. *Mary Poppins* (1964), D. *Rosemary's Baby* (Ira Levin, 1968), A. *A Clockwork Orange* (Anthony Burgess, 1971).
7. False. Heller had long been dissatisfied with any attempt to adapt his novel for the big screen, famously resisting even Orson Welles' attempt to buy the rights in the early 1960s.
8. A. *Fight Club. American Psycho* was based on a book by Brett Easton Ellis, *Requiem for a Dream,* a book by Hubert Selby Jr., and *Trainspotting,* a novel by Irvine Welsh.
9. B. *Alice in Wonderland*. It is Lewis Carroll's book that dates from 1865; J.M. Barrie's *Peter Pan* was originally a play written in 1904, Dodie Smith's *One Hundred and One Dalmatians* was published in 1956, and Rudyard Kipling's *The Jungle Book* dates from 1894.
10. D. *Patriot Games. Patriot Games* was a novel by Tom Clancy.
11. B. Willy Wonka. Gene Wilder starred as Willy Wonka in the original 1971 adaptation of *Charlie and the Chocolate Factory*, Johnny Depp took over the role in Tim Burton's 2005 version, and Timothée Chalamet played the character in the 2023 prequel, *Wonka*.
12. C. Albert Finney. Richard Widmark played the victim in the film, while Peter Ustinov played Poirot on film three times, in *Death on the Nile* (1978), *Evil Under the Sun* (1982), and *Appointment with Death* (1988). Kenneth Branagh recently revived the character in another adaptation of *Murder on the Orient Express* in 2017.
13. B. Count Dracula. Sherlock Holmes is a close second, with around 250 movie appearances.

14. C. *Misery*. Caan plays an author trapped in a psychopathic fan's home after a car accident.
15. B. *Schindler's List*. *Schindler's List* was based on Keneally's 1982 novel *Schindler's Ark*. *The Hours* was written by Michael Cunningham, *The Remains of the Day* by Kazuo Ishiguro, and *The English Patient* by Michael Ondaatje.
16. False. The final *Harry Potter* movie grossed more — around $1.3 billion — in 2011.
17. B. Kiefer Sutherland. Kiefer's father Donald Sutherland played President Coriolanus Snow in the *Hunger Games* movies.
18. A. William Shakespeare. Stephen King is said to be the most adapted living author, but Shakespeare is by far the most adapted writer of all time.

DID YOU KNOW?

When adjusted for inflation, *Gone with the Wind* remains not just the highest-grossing literary adaptation in cinema history but the highest-grossing movie of all time: in modern terms, it made the equivalent of $4.3 billion.

CHAPTER 27
THE BRITISH ARE COMING!

From Charlie Chaplin to Alfred Hitchcock, some of cinema's greatest stars and pioneers were British. We're hopping across the Atlantic for this next set of questions, all about British actors, actresses, and films.

1. Which star of the Daniel Craig-era of *Bond* movies provides the voice of Paddington Bear in the big-screen adventures?

   a. Colin Firth
   b. Ralph Fiennes
   c. Ben Whishaw
   d. Jonathan Bailey

2. What genre are the classic British *Carry On* films?

   a. Action adventure
   b. Comedy
   c. Costume drama
   d. Biopic

3. Who played serial killer John Christie in the 1971 true crime drama *10 Rillington Place*?

   a. Ben Kingsley
   b. Peter O'Toole
   c. Richard Attenborough
   d. Michael Caine

4. Which of these British romantic comedies was not written by screenwriter Richard Curtis?

   a. *Notting Hill*
   b. *Four Weddings and a Funeral*
   c. *Love Actually*
   d. *The Holiday*

5. To what Italian city does the bereaved couple at the center of the 1973 thriller *Don't Look Now* travel?

   a. Rome
   b. Milan
   c. Florence
   d. Venice

6. What kind of animal features in the 1969 British drama *Kes*?

   a. Fish
   b. Bird

c. Cat

d. Horse

7. The 1946 British fantasy drama *Stairway to Heaven*, starring David Niven, is set during which conflict?

    a. Wars of the Roses

    b. English Civil War

    c. Napoleonic War

    d. World War II

8. Which legendary English actor played multiple roles in the 1949 comedy *Kind Hearts and Coronets*?

    a. Alex Guinness

    b. Peter O'Toole

    c. Richard Harris

    d. Ralph Richardson

9. True or False? Ewan McGregor made his big-screen debut in the grimy 1996 drama *Trainspotting*.

10. Who starred in the classic British comedy *Withnail & I*?

    a. John Cleese

    b. Richard E. Grant

    c. Jim Broadbent

    d. Ian Holm

11. Which British director's movies *The Wind That Shakes the Barley* and *I, Daniel Blake* both won the coveted Palme d'Or at the Cannes Film Festival?

    a. Danny Boyle

    b. Ken Loach

    c. Sam Mendes

    d. Ken Russell

12. Which Oscar-winning actor directed the acclaimed 1997 British drama *Nil By Mouth*?

    a. Bob Hoskins

    b. Gary Oldman

    c. Colin Firth

    d. Jeremy Irons

13. What is the name of the island on which the classic 1973 British folk horror *The Wicker Man* is set?

   a. Winterisle
   b. Springisle
   c. Summerisle
   d. Autumnisle

14. True or False? The acclaimed 1946 adaptation of Charles Dickens' *Great Expectations* was the first Dickens adaptation to win Best Picture at the Oscars.

15. The 1960 British movie *Peeping Tom* was controversial because of its portrayal of what?

   a. A stripper
   b. A spy
   c. A serial killer
   d. A single father

16. Put these British actors in order from oldest to youngest.

   a. John Gielgud
   b. Patrick Stewart
   c. Helen Mirren
   d. Maggie Smith

17. Who directed the 1938 British thriller *The Lady Vanishes*?

   a. David Lean
   b. John Schlesinger
   c. Alfred Hitchcock
   d. Richard Attenborough

18. The 1971 Michael Caine movie *Get Carter* is what genre of film?

   a. Slasher
   b. Gangster
   c. Tearjerker
   d. Slapstick comedy

ANSWERS

1. C. Ben Whishaw. Colin Firth was originally cast as Paddington, but Whishaw later took over the role.
2. B. Comedy. The series has included some biopics and costume dramas over the years, but the *Carry On* franchise was a series of bawdy comedies.
3. C. Richard Attenborough. Christie was a notorious serial murderer in 1940s London.
4. D. *The Holiday*. Curtis also adapted the first two Bridget Jones movies and co-wrote the two Mr. Bean movies.
5. D. Venice. Adapted from a short story by Daphne du Maurier, the film starred Donald Sutherland and Julie Christie.
6. B. Bird. The film follows a young boy from a working-class family who raises a fledgling kestrel and learns the art of falconry.
7. D. World War II. Niven starred as an RAF pilot in the movie, which was set at the very end of the war in 1945.
8. A. Alec Guinness. Guinness played all the members of the aristocratic D'Ascoyne family in the movie.
9. False. McGregor made his debut in the drama *Being Human* in 1994.
10. B. Richard E. Grant. The movie also starred *Doctor Who* actor Paul McGann and future *Harry Potter* actor Richard Griffiths.
11. B. Ken Loach. Loach's other movies include *Looking for Eric, The Old Oak, Fatherland,* and *My Name is Joe.*
12. B. Gary Oldman. The movie was Oldman's directorial debut.
13. C. Summerisle. The film starred Christopher Lee as the leader of a Celtic pagan cult.
14. False. The movie was nominated for Best Picture but lost out to the Gregory Peck drama *Gentleman's Agreement.*
15. C. A serial killer. The movie starred the German actor Karlheinz Böhm as a serial killer who films women as they are murdered.
16. A. John Gielgud (1904), D. Maggie Smith (1934), B. Patrick Stewart (1940), C. Helen Mirren (1945).
17. C. Alfred Hitchcock. The movie's success was instrumental in paving Hitchcock's move to Hollywood soon afterward.
18. B. Gangster. The movie was a revenge drama, starring Caine as a London gangster who returns to his hometown after his brother's death.

DID YOU KNOW?

The highest-grossing fully British-made movie of all time is *Four Weddings and a Funeral*, which grossed over £200 million ($250 million) in 1994.

CHAPTER 28
SUPERHEROES

Thanks to the likes of the Marvel Cinematic Universe and the *Avengers* franchise, there are often multiple superhero movies released each year — some of which are name-checked in this next set of questions!

1. Released in May 2008, what was the first movie in the Marvel Cinematic Universe?

    a. *Thor*
    b. *Iron Man*
    c. *The Avengers*
    d. *Captain America: The First Avenger*

2. Which cast member of the 2022 movie *Black Panther: Wakanda Forever* was nominated for an Oscar for her role in the film?

    a. Lupita Nyong'o
    b. Letitia Wright
    c. Angela Bassett
    d. Danai Gurira

3. Who stars in the *Venom* series of movies?

    a. Tom Hardy
    b. Tobey Maguire
    c. Andrew Garfield
    d. Tom Holland

4. The 2017 movie *Logan* is part of what superhero franchise?

    a. *Batman*
    b. *X-Men*
    c. *Superman*
    d. *The Incredible Hulk*

5. True or False? Before Christopher Reeve was cast in the original *Superman* movie in 1978, the role was offered to Paul Newman.

6. Put these superhero movies of the 2010s in order, starting with the earliest:

    a. *Spider-Man: Into the Spider-Verse*
    b. *Megamind*
    c. *The Dark Knight Rises*
    d. *Ant-Man*

7. Who played the antagonist The Scarecrow in the 2015 movie *Batman Begins*?

a. Gary Oldman
b. Cillian Murphy
c. Tom Wilkinson
d. Liam Neeson

8. In what year was Patty Jenkins' second *Wonder Woman* movie set?

a. 1974
b. 1949
c. 1984
d. 1989

9. What is the family surname of *The Incredibles* in the 2004 Pixar movie?

a. Parr
b. Pratt
c. Potts
d. Price

10. In what decade did Batman make his first appearance on film?

a. 1930s
b. 1940s
c. 1950s
d. 1960s

11. In what MCU movie did Tom Holland make his first appearance as Spider-Man?

a. *Iron Man 2*
b. *Thor*
c. *Avengers: Age of Ultron*
d. *Captain America: Civil War*

12. Who played the villain Laurel Hedare opposite Halle Berry in the 2004 *Catwoman* movie?

a. Sharon Stone
b. Demi Moore
c. Alicia Silverstone
d. Meg Ryan

13. True or False? Before Jack Nicholson was cast in the role, John Lithgow was approached to play the Joker in Tim Burton's 1989 *Batman* movie.

14. Put these X-Men movies in order, starting with the earliest:

a. *X-Men: The Last Stand*
b. *X-Men: Days of Future Past*
c. *X-Men Origins: Wolverine*
d. *X-Men: First Class*

15. In what year was the first *Guardians of the Galaxy* movie, *Vol. 1*, released?

    a. 2011
    b. 2014
    c. 2017
    d. 2020

16. Who played Lex Luthor in the original *Superman* movies starring Christopher Reeve?

    a. Jack Nicholson
    b. Jon Voight
    c. Gene Hackman
    d. James Wood

17. Which of these actresses appeared in the first *Doctor Strange* movie opposite Benedict Cumberbatch in 2016?

    a. Tilda Swinton
    b. Emma Thompson
    c. Julianne Moore
    d. Keira Knightley

18. True or False? The third *Deadpool* movie, *Deadpool & Wolverine*, broke the record as the highest-grossing R-rated movie of all time.

ANSWERS

1. B. *Iron Man*. Phase One of the MCU included all four of these movies, plus 2008's *The Incredible Hulk* and 2010's sequel *Iron Man 2*.
2. C. Angela Bassett. The movie earned Bassett her second career Oscar nomination.
3. A. Tom Hardy. The other answers here are all Spider-Man actors.
4. B. *X-Men*. The movie was the tenth film in the *X-Men* series, the third Wolverine movie.
5. True. In fact, Newman was offered the part of Superman, then Lex Luther, and Jor-El, Superman's father, but turned all three down.
6. B. *Megamind* (2010), C. *The Dark Knight Rises* (2012), D. *Ant-Man* (2015), A. *Spider-Man: Into the Spider-Verse* (2018).
7. B. Cillian Murphy. Oldman plays Inspector Jim Gordon, Tom Wilkinson, mob boss Carmine Falcone, and Liam Neeson, Ra's al Ghul.
8. C. 1984. *Wonder Woman 1984* was released in 2020 and starred Gal Gadot as the eponymous heroine.
9. A. Parr. Mr. Incredible and Elastigirl are the heads of the Parr family.
10. B. 1940s. More than 20 years before Adam West starred as Batman in the 1960s, Columbia Pictures released a 15-chapter serial film called *Batman* in 1943 starring Lewis Wilson.
11. D. *Captain America: Civil War*. Holland made a brief appearance at the end of the second *Captain America* movie in 2016.
12. A. Sharon Stone. Halle Berry was awarded the Golden Raspberry for Worst Actress for *Catwoman*—an award she accepted in person, taking her 2001 Oscar with her!
13. True. Lithgow reportedly didn't understand the scope and importance of the project and talked Burton out of hiring him!
14. A. *X-Men: The Last Stand* (2006), C. *X-Men Origins: Wolverine* (2009), D. *X-Men: First Class* (2011), B. *X-Men: Days of Future Past* (2014).
15. B. 2014. It was followed by *Vol. 2* in 2017 and *Vol. 3* in 2023.
16. C. Gene Hackman. The film starred two Oscar-winning legends, with Marlon Brando taking the role of Jor-El, Superman's father.
17. A. Tilda Swinton. Swinton played the Ancient One in the film and reprised the role in the 2019 film *Avengers: Endgame*.
18. True. The film grossed $1.3 billion at the box office.

DID YOU KNOW?

Six of the top 25 highest-grossing movies of all time are superhero movies, with the Marvel Cinematic Universe alone now having grossed over $9 billion at the box office.

CHAPTER 29
SPORTS ON THE SILVER SCREEN

From reenactments of famous moments to biopics and original stories, some of the most popular and successful sporting movies of all time feature in this next set of questions.

1. While Robert De Niro starred as Jake LaMotta in Martin Scorsese's *Raging Bull*, who played his younger brother Joey?

    a. Ray Liotta
    b. Joe Pesci
    c. Paul Sorvino
    d. Andy García

2. What sport was featured in the 2024 movie *Challengers*, starring Zendaya, Mike Faist, and Josh O'Connor?

    a. Tennis
    b. Baseball
    c. Swimming
    d. Hockey

3. What city does Rocky Balboa come from in the boxing movie franchise?

    a. Chicago
    b. Philadelphia
    c. San Francisco
    d. Miami

4. Who starred opposite Kevin Costner in the 1988 baseball comedy *Bull Durham*?

    a. Geena Davis
    b. Madonna
    c. Rosanna Arquette
    d. Susan Sarandon

5. What sport featured in the 1996 sports movie *Tin Cup*?

    a. Boxing
    b. Rowing
    c. Golf
    d. Archery

6. In the 1993 comedy *Cool Runnings*, which unlikely country sends a bobsleigh team to the 1988 Winter Olympics in Calgary?

    a. Jamaica
    b. Nigeria

c. Malaysia

d. Kenya

7. In which decade was the classic British sports drama *Chariots of Fire* set?

a. 1890s

b. 1920s

c. 1940s

d. 1960s

8. True or False? The 1994 basketball drama *Blue Chips* featured Shaquille O'Neal among its cast.

9. Who directed the 1999 football drama *Any Given Sunday*?

a. Oliver Stone

b. Steven Spielberg

c. Robert Zemeckis

d. Michael Mann

10. Put these 21st-century sporting biopics in order, starting with the earliest:

a. *The Fighter*

b. *I, Tonya*

c. *Rush*

d. *Nyad*

11. Who won an Oscar for her role as a female boxer in *Million Dollar Baby*?

a. Halle Berry

b. Charlize Theron

c. Sandra Bullock

d. Hilary Swank

12. What sport features in the 2009 movie *Invictus*?

a. Rugby

b. Athletics

c. Soccer

d. Water polo

13. Who starred as British Formula 1 driver James Hunt in Ron Howard's 2018 movie *Rush*?

a. Chris Hemsworth

b. Christian Bale

    c. Sam Rockwell

    d. Clive Owen

14. Which of these future Oscar nominees starred in the 2002 British sports comedy *Bend It Like Beckham*?

    a. Kate Winslet

    b. Emily Blunt

    c. Keira Knightley

    d. Felicity Jones

15. Which legendary soccer star played Corporal Luis Fernandez in John Huston's World War II movie *Victory*?

    a. Pelé

    b. Didi

    c. Ronaldo

    d. Garrincha

16. Who starred as Randy "The Ram" Robinson in Darren Aronofsky's Oscar-nominated 2008 sports drama *The Wrestler*?

    a. Bruce Willis

    b. Mickey Rourke

    c. Willem Dafoe

    d. Sylvester Stallone

17. What sport featured in the 1966 documentary *The Endless Summer*?

    a. Cricket

    b. Polo

    c. Surfing

    d. Golf

18. Who starred as baseball legend Lou Gehrig in the 1942 drama *The Pride of the Yankees*?

    a. Clint Eastwood

    b. Gary Cooper

    c. James Stewart

    d. Cary Grant

ANSWERS

1. B. Joe Pesci. Pesci was nominated for the Supporting Actor Oscar for his performance.
2. A. Tennis. The movie followed a love triangle between the three leads, set across a decade of their careers.
3. B. Philadelphia. The first movie features a scene in which Rocky runs up the steps of the Philadelphia Museum of Art.
4. D. Susan Sarandon. Sarandon played a baseball groupie who falls for veteran catcher Crash Davis, played by Costner.
5. C. Golf. *Tin Cup* reunited Kevin Costner with filmmaker Rob Shelton, who had written and directed *Bull Durham*.
6. A. Jamaica. The film featured legendary comedy actor John Candy as a former Olympic bobsledder who is roped in to coach the Jamaican side.
7. B. 1920s. The movie told the story of two competing runners at the 1924 Paris Olympics.
8. True. The movie starred Nick Nolte as a high school coach attempting to put a team together, with O'Neal playing one of the students.
9. A. Oliver Stone. The film featured an all-star cast, including Al Pacino, Dennis Quaid, James Woods, Jamie Foxx, and Cameron Diaz.
10. A. *The Fighter* (2010), C. *Rush* (2013), B. *I, Tonya* (2017), D. *Nyad* (2023).
11. D. Hilary Swank. Swank played impoverished amateur-turned-pro boxer Maggie Fitzgerald in the film, winning the 2004 Best Actress Oscar.
12. A. Rugby. The movie told the story of Nelson Mandela's attempt to improve South Africa's chances in the 1995 Rugby World Cup.
13. A. Chris Hemsworth. The movie also featured Daniel Brühl as Austrian F1 driver Niki Lauda, who was Hunt's main rival.
14. C. Keira Knightley. Knightley played a member of an all-female football team in London who encourages a local Punjabi girl to try out.
15. A. Pelé. The 1981 movie (which was also titled *Escape to Victory*) told the story of a group of prisoners of war who use a soccer game as an opportunity to escape.
16. B. Mickey Rourke. Rourke was nominated for Best Actor for his performance.
17. C. Surfing. The movie followed a group of Californian surfers as they tour the world.

18. B. Gary Cooper. The movie told of legendary Yankees first-baseman Lou Gehrig, who died of motor neuron disease at 37.

DID YOU KNOW?

When *Rocky* won Best Picture at the Oscars in 1977, it was the first sports movie to win the title in the award's history!

CHAPTER 30
HORROR MOVIES

From ghosts and creature features to the blood-and-guts video nasties, horror movies have kept us on the edges of our seats — or with our hands over our eyes! — since the very earliest days of cinema.

1. Which legendary actor starred as Father Merrin in William Friedkin's *The Exorcist*?

    a. Max von Sydow
    b. Vincent Price
    c. John Lithgow
    d. Charles Grodin

2. What kind of giant mutant creature terrorized a New York apartment block in the 2021 movie *Sting*?

    a. Bee
    b. Snake
    c. Spider
    d. Octopus

3. Adapted from a Stephen King story, much of the action in the 2007 horror movie *The Mist* takes place where?

    a. A supermarket
    b. A lighthouse
    c. A library
    d. A police station

4. Who played the first on-screen victim of the ghostface killer in the 1996 slasher horror *Scream*?

    a. Courtney Cox
    b. Drew Barrymore
    c. Neve Campbell
    d. Rose McGowen

5. True or False? Prior to writing *The Exorcist*, the author and screenwriter William Peter Blatty was best known as a comedy writer.

6. Put these creepy creature features in order, starting with the earliest:

    a. *Tremors*
    b. *The Creature from the Black Lagoon*
    c. *Alien*
    d. *Anaconda*

180

7. Who starred as a woman impregnated by the Devil in the 1968 occult horror *Rosemary's Baby*?

   a. Sissy Spacek
   b. Mia Farrow
   c. Shirley MacLaine
   d. Ava Gardner

8. What kind of creature features in the 1955 monster movie *It Came from Beneath the Sea*?

   a. Shark
   b. Sea snake
   c. Octopus
   d. Crocodile

9. *The Blair Witch Project* is popularly said to have sparked the 21st century's fondness for found-footage horror movies. In what year was it released?

   a. 1999
   b. 2001
   c. 2003
   d. 2005

10. *The Ring* series of movies is based on an original film from what country?

    a. India
    b. Japan
    c. Ireland
    d. Italy

11. What classic 1992 horror was based on Clive Barker's short story *The Forbidden*?

    a. *Candyman*
    b. *Jacob's Ladder*
    c. *Nightbreed*
    d. *I Know What You Did Last Summer*

12. In what year was the first *Paranormal Activity* movie released?

    a. 2004
    b. 2007
    c. 2010
    d. 2013

13. Put these gruesome 1980s horrors in order, starting with the earliest:

    a. *Re-Animator*
    b. *Videodrome*
    c. *The Blob*
    d. *Scanners*

14. True or False? Alfred Hitchcock's *Psycho* was the first Hollywood film to show someone taking a shower.

15. The Icelandic actor Gunnar Hansen is best known for his work in what classic horror movie?

    a. *An American Werewolf in London*
    b. *The Texas Chainsaw Massacre*
    c. *Nightmare on Elm Street*
    d. *Night of the Living Dead*

16. In what decade was the first *Godzilla* movie released?

    a. 1940s
    b. 1950s
    c. 1960s
    d. 1970s

17. Which of these items is used to gruesome effect in the 1990 Stephen King adaptation *Misery*?

    a. Chainsaw
    b. Sledgehammer
    c. Nail gun
    d. Vice

18. True or False? The owners of Oregon's Timberline Lodge, which served as the Overlook Hotel in Stanley Kubrick's adaptation of *The Shining*, personally requested the film's screenplay focus the spooky action in Room 237, not Room 217 as it had been in the book.

ANSWERS

1. A. Max von Sydow. Besides his iconic role in *The Exorcist*, 21st-century audiences will know Max Von Sydow from his appearances in *Minority Report, Shutter Island*, and *Star Wars*.
2. C. Spider. The movie told the story of an alien arachnid that makes a home for itself in the air vents of an apartment block.
3. A. A supermarket. Directed by Frank Darabont, *The Mist* has become infamous for its bleak ending, which Darabont added to the King story himself.
4. B. Drew Barrymore. The movie starred all four of these actresses, but it was Barrymore's character Casey who is memorably slain (along with her boyfriend) in the movie's opening scene.
5. True. Before *The Exorcist*, Blatty wrote the Danny Kaye comedy *The Man from the Diners' Club* and the *Pink Panther* sequel *A Shot in the Dark*.
6. B. *The Creature from the Black Lagoon* (1954), C. *Alien* (1979), A. *Tremors* (1990), D. *Anaconda* (1997).
7. B. Mia Farrow. The movie was adapted from a 1967 novel by Ira Levin.
8. C. Octopus. The film features a giant octopus that becomes radioactive due to nuclear testing.
9. A. 1999. *The Blair Witch Project* is also widely held to be the most profitable movie ever made; shot on a budget of $35,000, it earned $250 million at the box office.
10. B. Japan. The first Japanese Ring movie, *Ringu*, was released in 1998, while the franchise itself is based on a 1991 novel by Koji Suzuki.
11. A. *Candyman*. Barker's original story, which was set in the UK, was relocated to Chicago in the movie.
12. B. 2007. The seventh movie in the series, *Next of Kin*, was released in 2021.
13. D. *Scanners* (1981), B. *Videodrome* (1983), A. *Re-Animator* (1985), C. *The Blob* (1988).
14. False. It was, however, the first film to show a flushing toilet!
15. B. *The Texas Chainsaw Massacre*. It was Hansen who was behind the mask as Leatherface in the notorious 1974 movie.
16. B. 1950s. The original Japanese *Godzilla*, directed by Ishiro Honda, was released in 1954.

17. B. Sledgehammer. The sledgehammer scene was named as the twelfth scariest movie moment of all time in a 2004 survey by Bravo.
18. True. The change was requested as the Timberline had no room 237, but it did have a 217 — and the owners were worried guests would refuse to stay in the room!

DID YOU KNOW?

The scene in *The Shining* in which Shelley Duvall holds Jack Nicholson back with a baseball bat took 127 takes!

CHAPTER 31
STEVEN SPIELBERG

With a filmography including the likes of *Jaws*, *Jurassic Park*, and *Saving Private Ryan*, few directors have left a mark on the movie landscape like Steven Spielberg. These next questions celebrate his exceptional moviemaking.

1. In what year did *Jaws* first terrify cinema audiences?

    a. 1971
    b. 1975
    c. 1979
    d. 1984

2. Who does *Seinfeld* actor Wayne Knight play in *Jurassic Park*?

    a. Ian Malcolm
    b. Dennis Nedry
    c. John Hammond
    d. Alan Grant

3. Who starred as Maria in Steven Spielberg's 2021 adaptation of *West Side Story*?

    a. Ariana DeBose
    b. Rachel Zegler
    c. Zendaya
    d. Selena Gomez

4. What is the name of the ten-year-old boy who befriends the eponymous alien in *E.T. The Extra Terrestrial*?

    a. Elliott
    b. Ethan
    c. Ezra
    d. Emmett

5. Who starred as Frank Abagnale Jr. in *Catch Me If You Can*?

    a. Tom Hardy
    b. Sean Penn
    c. Leonardo DiCaprio
    d. Matt Damon

6. True or False? Several of Steven Spielberg's movies have been named Best Picture at the Oscars, but he has never been named Best Director.

7. Put these Spielberg blockbusters in order, starting with the earliest:

a. *Hook*
b. *Raiders of the Lost Ark*
c. *Ready Player One*
d. *Close Encounters of the Third Kind*

8. Who played Abraham Lincoln in Spielberg's *Lincoln*?

    a. Adrian Brody
    b. Gary Oldman
    c. Christian Bale
    d. Daniel Day-Lewis

9. The 2015 Spielberg drama *Bridge of Spies* was set in what time period?

    a. The American Civil War
    b. The Spanish Civil War
    c. The Cold War
    d. The Gulf War

10. Who provided the voice of Tintin in Spielberg's 2011 animated movie *The Adventures of Tintin*?

    a. Tom Holland
    b. Freddie Highmore
    c. Nicholas Hoult
    d. Jamie Bell

11. Spielberg's 2001 science fiction epic *A.I. Artificial Intelligence* was originally intended to be directed by, and is dedicated to, which fellow filmmaker?

    a. Tony Scott
    b. Stanley Kubrick
    c. Robert Altman
    d. Billy Wilder

12. True or False? Spielberg's 1985 adaptation of Alice Walker's novel *The Color Purple* did not win a single Oscar from its 11 nominations.

13. Who starred as Katharine Graham, the publisher of the *Washington Post*, in Spielberg's 2017 political thriller, *The Post*?

    a. Meryl Streep
    b. Glenn Close
    c. Laura Dern
    d. Vera Farmiga

14. Who narrated Steven Spielberg's adaptation of *The War of the Worlds*?

    a. Ian McKellen
    b. Denzel Washington
    c. Patrick Stewart
    d. Morgan Freeman

15. Which legendary filmmaker had a cameo role in Spielberg's semi-autobiographical movie *The Fabelmans*, playing equally legendary director John Ford?

    a. David Lynch
    b. Clint Eastwood
    c. Mel Brooks
    d. Sydney Pollack

16. What Spielberg movie was an adaptation of a story by Michael Morpurgo?

    a. *Minority Report*
    b. *Jurassic Park*
    c. *The BFG*
    d. *War Horse*

17. What classic Spielberg movie famously features a camera technique called the dolly zoom?

    a. *Indiana Jones and the Temple of Doom*
    b. *Saving Private Ryan*
    c. *The Lost World: Jurassic Park*
    d. *Jaws*

18. Put these lesser-known Spielberg movies in order, starting with the earliest:

    a. *1941*
    b. *The Terminal*
    c. *Empire of the Sun*
    d. *The Sugarland Express*

ANSWERS

1. B. 1975. *Jaws* is often cited as the first modern summer blockbuster, having been released in June 1975.
2. B. Dennis Nedry. It is head computer programmer Nedry who takes the park's security systems offline in order to steal dinosaur embryos.
3. B. Rachel Zegler. DeBose plays Anita in the movie and won an Oscar for her performance.
4. A. Elliott. Played by Henry Thomas, Elliott is the middle child of the Taylor family.
5. C. Leonardo DiCaprio. The movie also starred Tom Hanks as FBI agent Carl Hanratty and Christopher Walken as Frank Abagnale Sr.
6. False. Actually, Spielberg won the Best Director award for *Schindler's List* and *Saving Private Ryan*.
7. D. *Close Encounters of the Third Kind* (1977), B. *Raiders of the Lost Ark* (1984), A. *Hook* (1991), C. *Ready Player One* (2018).
8. D. Daniel Day-Lewis. The movie earned Day-Lewis his record-breaking third Best Actor Oscar.
9. C. The Cold War. The movie starred Tom Hanks as a lawyer overseeing the exchange of two Cold War-era spies.
10. D. Jamie Bell. *Billy Elliot* and *King Kong* star Bell starred alongside fellow *King Kong* castmate Andy Serkis as Captain Haddock.
11. B. Stanley Kubrick. Having spent two decades on it, Kubrick handed his *A.I.* project to Spielberg in 1995. He completed the movies after Kubrick's death four years later.
12. True. Eleven remains the record for the most Oscar nominations without a single win.
13. A. Meryl Streep. The movie told the story of a group of *Washington Post* journalists attempting to publish the Pentagon Papers.
14. D. Morgan Freeman. The narrator bookends the movie, explaining the role and downfall of the extraterrestrial life in the film.
15. A. David Lynch. It was Lynch's final acting role before his death in 2025.
16. D. *War Horse*. *Minority Report* was a story by Philip K. Dick, *Jurassic Park* was written by Michael Crichton, and *The BFG* was a children's book by Roald Dahl.
17. D. *Jaws*. The dolly zoom was used to memorable effect in *Jaws*, as the camera zooms in on Chief Brody as he sees a child killed by the shark in the water before him.

18. D. *The Sugarland Express* (1974), A. *1941* (1979), C. *Empire of the Sun* (1987), B. *The Terminal* (2004).

DID YOU KNOW?

Spielberg is officially the most bankable director in Hollywood history, with a total box office gross across his career now exceeding $10 billion!

CHAPTER 32
OSCAR SEASON

The Oscars are watched by hundreds of millions of movie fans the world over. Some of the awards' most famous wins, losses, and records are dealt with in these next questions.

1. Which of these was not one of the 11 awards won from a record 14 nominations by *Titanic* at the 1998 Oscars?

   a. Best Picture
   b. Best Director, James Cameron
   c. Best Actress, Kate Winslet
   d. Best Song, "My Heart Will Go On"

2. No movie that won Best Picture at the Oscars in the entire 20th century had a title beginning with N. In the first two decades of the 21st century, there were two. Name either of them.

3. Who received his record 54th Oscar nomination in 2023?

   a. Steven Spielberg
   b. Aaron Sorkin
   c. John Williams
   d. Woody Allen

4. The Oscar-winning song "Take My Breath Away" featured on the soundtrack to what 1980s blockbuster?

   a. *Dirty Dancing*
   b. *Top Gun*
   c. *Working Girl*
   d. *An Officer and a Gentleman*

5. Which two legendary performers tied in the 1969 Best Actress Oscar vote?

   a. Katharine Hepburn and Barbra Streisand
   b. Audrey Hepburn and Bette Davis
   c. Maggie Smith and Peggy Ashcroft
   d. Elizabeth Taylor and Vanessa Redgrave

6. Who is the only person in history to have been posthumously nominated for more than one Oscar?

   a. Alec Guinness
   b. Peter Finch
   c. James Dean
   d. Heath Ledger

7. Put these early Best Picture winners in order, starting with the earliest:

    a. *The Lost Weekend*
    b. *The Greatest Show on Earth*
    c. *How Green Was My Valley*
    d. *You Can't Take It with You*

8. In what year did Katharine Hepburn receive the first of her four Oscars?

    a. 1933
    b. 1943
    c. 1953
    d. 1963

9. In 2009, the Academy increased the number of movies eligible for Best Picture nominations from five to how many?

    a. Eight
    b. Ten
    c. 12
    d. 15

10. Edith Head received 35 Oscar nominations throughout her career — in what category?

    a. Editing
    b. Costume design
    c. Cinematography
    d. Sound mixing

11. True or False? In the early decades of the Academy Awards, there were separate Best Picture Oscars recognizing black and white and color movies.

12. As well as winning 11 Oscars throughout his career, Cedric Gibbons achieved a unique place in Oscar history for what reason?

    a. He designed the Oscar statuette
    b. He founded the Academy
    c. He presented the first Oscars ceremony
    d. He was the first person to win more than one award at the same ceremony

13. Throughout the Oscars' history, only three films have won the so-called "Big Five" awards — Best Picture, Director, Actor, Actress, and

Screenplay, either original or adapted — in a single night. Name one of them.

14. Which of these classic 1980s hits did not win the Academy Award for Best Original Song?

    a. "I Just Called to Say I Love You"
    b. "9 to 5"
    c. "Flashdance ... What a Feeling"
    d. "Say You, Say Me"

15. What was the first sequel to win the Academy Award for Best Animated Feature?

    a. *Shrek 2*
    b. *Toy Story 3*
    c. *Kung Fu Panda 2*
    d. *Inside Out 2*

16. True or False? The Academy Award itself is surprisingly heavy and weighs in at around eight pounds.

17. All of these actors have won Oscars in non-acting categories. Put them in order of their non-acting win, starting with the one that occurred earliest:

    a. Robert Redford, Best Director
    b. Ben Affleck, Best Screenplay
    c. Brad Pitt, Best Picture producer
    d. Mel Gibson, Best Director

18. Which of these legendary Best Actor winners won their Oscar first?

    a. George C. Scott
    b. Paul Newman
    c. Jon Voight
    d. Rod Steiger

ANSWERS

1. C. Best Actress, Kate Winslet. Both Winslet and veteran actress Gloria Stewart—who played Winslet's character Rose as an old woman in the movie—were nominated for Oscars.
2. *No Country For Old Men* (in 2018) or *Nomadland* (in 2020).
3. C. John Williams. Composer Williams received the nomination for his score for the fifth Indiana Jones movie, *The Dial of Destiny*.
4. B. *Top Gun*. The song, performed by Berlin, won Oscars for its writers Giorgio Moroder (music) and Tom Whitlock (lyrics).
5. A. Katharine Hepburn and Barbra Streisand. Hepburn won for *The Lion in Winter*, and Streisand won for *Funny Girl*.
6. C. James Dean. Peter Finch won a posthumous Best Actor Academy Award for his role in *Network*, and Heath Ledger's Joker won him a posthumous Supporting Actor Oscar for *The Dark Knight*. But only James Dean achieved two posthumous nominations, for *East of Eden* in 1955 and *Giant* in 1956.
7. D. *You Can't Take It with You* (1938), C. *How Green Was My Valley* (1941), A. *The Lost Weekend* (1945), B. *The Greatest Show on Earth* (1952).
8. A. 1933. Hepburn first won for her role as Eva Lovelace in *Morning Glory*.
9. B. Ten. The decision came after several blockbusters missed out on Best Picture nominations.
10. B. Costume design. In a career spanning five decades, Head received 35 Oscar nominations, winning eight.
11. False. Some awards, such as costume design, were once divided into separate black-and-white and color categories, but Best Picture was not.
12. A. He designed the Oscar statuette. Gibbons' 11 Oscar wins came from a total of 39 career nominations.
13. *It Happened One Night* (1934), *One Flew Over the Cuckoo's Nest* (1975), or *The Silence of the Lambs* (1991).
14. B. "9 to 5." Dolly Parton was nominated for Best Song for "9 to 5" in 1980 but lost out to Irene Cara's hit "Fame."
15. B. *Toy Story 3*. All the movies here were nominated, but only *Toy Story 3* won the award, in 2010. (*Toy Story 4* went on to win it in 2019 too).
16. True. Oscars are made of bronze coated in solid gold and stand just over 13 inches tall.

17. A. Robert Redford, Best Director (*Ordinary People*, 1980), D. Mel Gibson, Best Director (*Braveheart*, 1995), B. Ben Affleck, Best Screenplay (*Good Will Hunting*, 1997, along with Matt Damon), C. Brad Pitt, Best Picture (*12 Years A Slave*, 2013).
18. D. Rod Steiger. Steiger won Best Actor for his role in 1967's *In the Heat of the Night*. George C. Scott won for *Patton* in 1970, Jon Voight for *Coming Home* in 1978, and Paul Newman for *The Color of Money* in 1986.

DID YOU KNOW?

No one knows how many Oscars are due to be handed out on Oscar night until the winning envelopes are opened. As a result, multiple Oscars are produced ahead of the ceremony, with any unused statuettes kept in storage until the following year.

CHAPTER 33
POP AND ROCK

From biopics to musicals, for as long as movies have had sound, music and musicians have appeared on screen. All the questions here in this penultimate chapter have to do with movie–music crossovers through the decades.

1. Which future director of *Superman II* and *Superman III* directed the Beatles' first two movies, *A Hard Day's Night* and *Help!*?

   a. Richard Lester
   b. Richard Donner
   c. Richard Attenborough
   d. Richard Wallace

2. In what year did the Spice Girls star in *Spice World: The Movie*?

   a. 1995
   b. 1997
   c. 1999
   d. 2001

3. True or False? Cher has been nominated for more acting Oscars than Original Song Oscars.

4. Which legendary rock star had an acting role in the movie *Fight Club*?

   a. Gene Simmons
   b. Meat Loaf
   c. Robert Plant
   d. Ozzy Osborne

5. What kind of supernatural being did David Bowie play in the 1983 thriller *The Hunger*?

   a. Vampire
   b. Werewolf
   c. Giant
   d. Poltergeist

6. What kind of film was Elvis Presley's big-screen debut, *Love Me Tender*?

   a. Western
   b. Thriller
   c. Gangster
   d. Heist

7. Who starred alongside Gene Kelly in the 1940s musicals *Anchors Aweigh, On the Town*, and *Take Me Out to the Ball Game*?

a. Dean Martin
b. Sammy Davis, Jr.
c. Frank Sinatra
d. Nat King Cole

8. Who directed Lady Gaga in the 2021 drama *House of Gucci*?

a. Todd Phillips
b. Ridley Scott
c. Ryan Murphy
d. Bradley Cooper

9. Which of these '90s movies did not star Jennifer Lopez?

a. *Anaconda*
b. *Out of Sight*
c. *Antz*
d. *Music of the Heart*

10. Which 2000s pop star made her feature film acting debut in the 2002 movie *Crossroads*?

a. Britney Spears
b. Christina Aguilera
c. Katy Perry
d. Avril Lavigne

11. Pop star Grace Jones played May Day in what 1980s Bond movie?

a. *A View to a Kill*
b. *The Living Daylights*
c. *Octopussy*
d. *Licence to Kill*

12. Beyoncé starred in the third movie in which series of comedy films?

a. *The Hangover*
b. *Anchorman*
c. *Austin Powers*
d. *American Pie*

13. Which legendary pop star appeared in David Cronenberg's *Videodrome*?

a. Debbie Harry
b. Annie Lennox
c. Madonna
d. Tina Turner

14. Who was responsible for the bestselling soundtrack album of the 1990s?

    a. Madonna
    b. Whitney Houston
    c. Mariah Carey
    d. Celine Dion

15. Rapper Eminem's movie *8 Mile* is set in what city?

    a. Milwaukee
    b. St. Louis
    c. Detroit
    d. Philadelphia

16. Which rock star has had roles in the movies *Precious, The Hunger Games,* and *Shotgun Wedding*?

    a. Lenny Kravitz
    b. Jon Bon Jovi
    c. Bruce Springsteen
    d. Alice Cooper

17. Who won great acclaim for her lead role in the Lars von Trier movie *Dancer in the Dark*?

    a. Björk
    b. Tori Amos
    c. P.J. Harvey
    d. Imogen Heap

18. True or False? Rock star Alanis Morissette played the Devil in Kevin Smith's 1999 comedy drama *Dogma*.

ANSWERS

1. A. Richard Lester. Although Richard Donner directed the first *Superman* movie in 1978, it was Richard Lester who directed the second and third movies, having established his career directing several Swinging Sixties movies.
2. B. 1997. The movie was released just 18 months after the Spice Girls burst onto the music scene with their debut hit "Wannabe" in the summer of 1996.
3. True. In fact, Cher's music has yet to receive a single Best Original Song nomination.
4. B. Meat Loaf. Meat Loaf played an overweight fighter in the eponymous club named Bob Paulson.
5. A. Vampire. Bowie played one half of a vampire couple in the film, alongside Catherine Deneuve.
6. A. Western. Set at the end of the Civil War, the movie was originally going to be called *The Reno Brothers* (with Elvis playing the youngest brother, Clint) before sales of Elvis' title song prompted it to be renamed.
7. C. Frank Sinatra. Sinatra starred in a slew of musicals in the 1940s and won an Oscar for his role in *From Here to Eternity* in 1953.
8. B. Ridley Scott. Bradley Cooper directed Gaga in *A Star is Born*, Todd Phillips directed her in *Joker: Folie à Deux*, and Ryan Murphy was the showrunner of *American Horror Story*.
9. D. *Music of the Heart*. Fellow Latin pop superstar Gloria Estefan appeared in this 1999 drama, alongside Meryl Streep and Angela Bassett.
10. A. Britney Spears. Britney's younger sister, Jamie Lynn Spears, played her character as a young girl in the movie.
11. A. *A View to a Kill*. Jones starred opposite Roger Moore as Bond and Christopher Walken as the villainous Max Zorin.
12. C. Austin Powers. Beyoncé played the sidekick Foxxy Cleopatra in 2002's *Goldmember*.
13. A. Debbie Harry. Blondie frontwoman Debbie Harry played radio host Nicki Brand in the film.
14. B. Whitney Houston. Houston's soundtrack to the 1992 movie *The Bodyguard* sold 45 million copies in the USA alone.
15. C. Detroit. Eminem starred as blue-collar factory worker Jimmy in the film, who raps under the name "B-Rabbit."

16. A. Lenny Kravitz. He has also appeared as himself in a handful of films, including the Ben Stiller comedy *Zoolander*.
17. A. Björk. Björk won the coveted Best Actress Award at the Cannes Film Festival in 2000 for her role in the film.
18. False. In fact, she played God!

DID YOU KNOW?

One of the first pop stars to earn an Oscar nomination was Doris Day in *Pillow Talk* in 1959.

CHAPTER 34
JUST FOR CINEPHILES!

For this final set of questions, we're upping the ante...Good luck!

1. Which of these characters is killed by the T-rex in Steven Spielberg's *Jurassic Park*?

   a. Robert Muldoon
   b. Dennis Nedry
   c. Ray Arnold
   d. Donald Gennaro

2. What did actor Barry Fitzgerald achieve at the 1944 Academy Awards for the movie *Going My Way*?

   a. Only non-speaking nomination
   b. Only actor also nominated for costume design
   c. Only Oscar-nominated performer never seen on screen
   d. Two acting nominations for the same performance

3. *Doctor Who* actor Peter Capaldi has also won an Oscar — in what category?

   a. Best Animated Feature
   b. Best Live Action Short Film
   c. Best Original Song
   d. Best Cinematography

4. Which of these was not one of the people who brought Darth Vader to life in the original *Star Wars* trilogy?

   a. James Earl Jones
   b. Sebastian Shaw
   c. Peter Mayhew
   d. David Prowse

5. True or False? Alfred Hitchcock's wife, Alma, was a successful Hollywood costume designer and makeup artist.

6. What color is the character Fear in the *Inside Out* movies?

   a. Blue
   b. Red
   c. Purple
   d. Green

7. Baz Luhrman's *Moulin Rouge!* is set across which two years?

   a. 1899–1900
   b. 1909–1910

c. 1919–1920
d. 1929–1930

8. All four of these actresses have appeared opposite Harrison Ford. Put their movie roles in order, starting with the one that appeared earliest:

a. Michelle Pfeiffer
b. Karen Allen
c. Kelly McGillis
d. Glenn Close

9. If all the Best Picture Oscar winners of the 20th century were put in alphabetical order, which of these actors starred in the movie that would come first?

a. Anthony Hopkins
b. Bette Davis
c. Christian Bale
d. Deborah Kerr

10. Which of these Oscar-winning movies of the 2000s is not set in California?

a. *There Will Be Blood*
b. *Sideways*
c. *No Country for Old Men*
d. *Wild*

11. True or False? The memorable final shot of the *Good Morning* tap dance routine in *Singin' in the Rain*—in which the three stars all somersault onto a couch before tipping over another—was filmed in a single take.

12. Michael Caine and Denzel Washington are two of only a handful of actors who have been nominated for an Oscar in how many consecutive decades?

a. Three
b. Four
c. Five
d. Six

13. What color dress does Marilyn Monroe wear to perform "Diamonds Are a Girl's Best Friend" in the 1953 movie *Gentlemen Prefer Blondes*?

a. Red
b. White

c. Pink

d. Yellow

14. The sounds made by a walrus, a tortoise, a horse, a dog, a dolphin, and a goose were all combined to make the on-screen sounds of+ what?

    a. The lightsabers in *Star Wars*
    b. The xenomorphs in *Alien*
    c. The flying monkeys in *The Wizard of Oz*
    d. The velociraptors in *Jurassic Park*

15. The Nicole Kidman horror *The Others* is set on what European island?

    a. Crete
    b. Jersey
    c. Sicily
    d. Isle of Wight

16. Put these musical numbers from *The Sound of Music* in the order that they're performed in the film:

    a. *Do-Re-Mi*
    b. *So Long, Farewell*
    c. *I Have Confidence*
    d. *My Favorite Things*

17. True or False? The largest amount of fake blood ever used in a movie was in the 2013 remake of *Evil Dead*.

18. Who or what in the history of Hollywood were Slats, Jackie, Tanner, George, and Leo?

    a. Placeholder names for unnamed characters in screenplays
    b. Names for mannequins used in stunts
    c. Alternative names for the Oscar statuette
    d. Roaring lions in the MGM logo

ANSWERS

1. D. Donald Gennaro. Played by *Miami Vice* actor Martin Ferrero, Donald Gennaro is the lawyer who is killed by the T-rex after it escapes its paddock.
2. D. Two acting nominations for the same performance. Due to a loophole in the Oscar nominations process at the time, Fitzgerald was nominated in both the Best Actor and Supporting Actor categories that year (winning the Supporting Actor award).
3. B. Best Live Action Short Film. Capaldi wrote and directed the short film *Franz Kafka's It's a Wonderful Life* in 1993.
4. C. Peter Mayhew. James Earl Jones voiced Darth Vader, David Prowse was inside his suit, and when Luke Skywalker removes his helmet at the end of *Return of the Jedi*, veteran stage actor Sebastian Shaw is inside.
5. False. In fact, she was a successful screenwriter and movie editor.
6. C. Purple. Fear, voiced by Bill Hader, is purple. Sadness is blue, Anger is red, and Disgust is green.
7. A. 1899–1900. The movie is split across the turn of the century.
8. B. Karen Allen (*Raiders of the Lost Ark*, 1981), C. Kelly McGillis (*Witness*, 1985), D. Glenn Close (*Air Force One*, 1997), A. Michelle Pfeiffer (*What Lies Beneath*, 2000).
9. B. Bette Davis. 1950's *All About Eve* would come first.
10. C. *No Country for Old Men*. It is set in Texas.
11. False. In fact, 40 takes were needed to get the stunt just right. By the end of the 14-hour day, Debbie Reynolds' feet were bleeding.
12. C. Five. Caine's nominations span the 1960s to the 2000s, while Denzel Washington has been nominated in every decade since the 1980s.
13. C. Pink. The shocking pink silk dress was designed by William Travilla.
14. D. The velociraptors in *Jurassic Park*. The velociraptor's bark is a mating tortoise, while the high-pitched scream that they make before attacking is a baby dolphin.
15. B. Jersey. The movie is set in 1945 on Jersey, the only British territory occupied by the Nazis during World War II.
16. C. *I Have Confidence*, D. *My Favorite Things*, A. *Do-Re-Mi*, B. *So Long, Farewell*.

17. False. Actually, the largest amount of fake blood ever used on screen was in a scene in *It Chapter Two* in 2019, in which Jessica Chastain's character is trapped in a bathroom stall flooded with 4,500 gallons of blood.
18. D. Roaring lions in the MGM logo. The famous MGM "roaring lion" logo has been used since the 1910s, with various individual lions — including all those here — filmed roaring in the central golden circle.

DID YOU KNOW?

On average, 7,000–10,000 films are produced every year.

CONCLUSION

Phew! And with that final batch of questions, *The Ultimate Movie Trivia Challenge* is complete.

So how did you score? You've faced a whopping 612 questions along the way, covering everything from the earliest silent movies to the Technicolor gaudiness of Hollywood's Golden Age and the superhero and fantasy epics of the 2000s and beyond. We've namechecked more than 200 movie stars, another 200 Oscar winners and nominees, and covered an entire century of filmmaking — so don't be too downhearted if you didn't score a perfect 612/612!

Along the way, hopefully you've not only put your film buff's knowledge to the test, but perhaps learned a little something you didn't know before — whether that's how they made the dinosaur sounds in Jurassic Park or how to do a dolly zoom camera trick!

But now, maybe it's time for a break? Hey — why not put a movie on?